DELFT CERAMICS

C. H. de Jonge

DELFT CERAMICS

PRAEGER PUBLISHERS

New York · Washington · London

PRAEGER PUBLISHERS, INC.
111 Fourth Avenue, New York, NY 10003, USA
5 Cromwell Place, London SW 7, England

Published in the United States of America in 1970
by Praeger Publishers, Inc.

Translated by Marie-Christine Hellin

Library of Congress Catalog Card Number: 68-24042

Printed in Austria

Contents

Foreword

In 1947 my book, *Oud-Nederlandsche Majolica en Delftsch Aardewerk*, written during the war years, was published by Scheltema en Holkema's Boekhandel en Uitgeversmaatschappij in Amsterdam. Since the war museums and collectors have again been able to give full attention to the ancient Delft potteries, and archivists and scholars have made significant advances in our knowledge. Outstanding among these researchers is Dr H. E. van Gelder who has demonstrated the crucial rôle played by the potters and the pottery painters in the development of high quality Delft ware and has shown that, although individual objects are often signed with the initials of the factory directors, these men were most commonly merely shareholders and not active artists. The greater knowledge of Delft which has accumulated during the past years demands a somewhat different treatment from my earlier study.

The present book is based on publications regarded as classic since the beginning of this century, such as those by Rackham, Neurdenburg and Hudig, and especially the notes of A. H. H. van der Burgh in the Gemeente Archief at Delft. These are now arranged in a card-index system and are an invaluable reference source. It is also based upon contemporary work in the field and, of course, upon the study of individual objects in museums and private collections.

The aim of this book is to present a scholarly, yet popular, survey of Delft faience which so far as possible treats of the less familiar pieces. Only brief attention is given to early Dutch majolica. There are sound reasons for this. During and after the war a tremendous number of new finds were made in this field and they must be considered in a proper study of the subject. Such a study is now in the capable hands of Dr A. Westers, director of the Groninger Museum voor Stad en Lande (whose as yet unpublished doctoral dissertation has given detailed attention to it) and of Dr I. P. J. Tichelaar, director of the Tichelaars Koninklyke Makkumse Aardewerken Tegelfabriek N. V. In this book, therefore, majolica is discussed only in broad terms and in connection with Delft faience.

The author of this book plans to publish in the near future a study of Dutch tiles and tile painting and this extensive subject is not treated in very great detail in this book. One reason for this is that the popular terminology 'Delft tiles' is at best misleading. This art form developed about 1600 in Rotterdam and the manufacture of tiles became widespread throughout the Netherlands; they were certainly made in Delft, notably at the potteries De Grieksche A and De Roos which produced unique objects in polychrome, black and gold, but Delft was merely one of many centres.

In the main, then, this book is a discussion of Delft faience which began to be differentiated from Dutch majolica in the second quarter of the seventeenth century and, for more than a hundred years thereafter, developed along many different lines. It is astonishing and fascinating to note that every phase of its development is accompanied by new refinements in technique and artistry.

I am greatly indebted to all who assisted me in the writing of this book. Dr Wester and Dr Tichelaar gave me all the help I desired, as did the authorities of the Rijksmuseum, the Museum Boymans-van Beuningen Het Prinsenhoff in Delft, the municipal museums in The Hague and Arnhem, the Victoria and Albert Museum, London and the Musées royaux d'Art and d'Histoire, Brussels. Both the Het Friesch Museum and Museum Het Princessehof in Leeuwarden, reorganized since the war, contain interesting pieces of Delft ware which I was able to view. I was also able to study several private collections in the Netherlands, chief among them that of the heirs of Dr F. H. Fentener van Vlissingen in Vught. And I must, of course, express my gratitude to my translator, Miss Marie-Christine Hellin.

Jonkvrouwe Dr C. H. de Jonge

The Hague, 1969

Introduction

Delft faience, often erroneously called Delft porcelain, developed out of Dutch majolica during the late Middle Ages. The ultimate place of origin is Italy, the most important centre for the manufacture of pottery during the fifteenth century. The word 'majolica' derives from Majorca, the port from which Spanish earthenwares were exported, but it soon became the collective term for all earthenware objects covered with a tin glaze. Spanish and Italian majolica had been sold in Flanders for decades, but direct Italian influence began in the early sixteenth century when Italian potters settled in the area (chiefly in Antwerp). The wars of the period caused many to emigrate again, this time to the northern Netherlands*, and in these provinces a more refined majolica was developed under their influence and Flemish-Dutch pottery emerged as an indigenous art. Haarlem, Amsterdam, Delft, Rotterdam and Gouda were the chief centres of this development.

The distinction between majolica and Delft faience (decorated tin-glazed earthenware the name of which is derived, via the French, from the Italian town of Faenza) begins in the very early seventeenth century when the Delft factories specialized in imitating the Chinese wares, which had begun to be imported in great quantities. Potteries in Delft and Haarlem, as well as attempting to copy Chinese decorative motifs and colouring, concentrated on problems of clay composition in an effort to produce a material as fine as porcelain. During this period Delft ware became known as both 'faience' and 'porcelain'. In 1648 the Hof van Holland, the highest court of the province of Holland, tried to clear up the dual terminology with its decrees on the 'new invention'. (A 'true' or 'hard' European porcelain was impossible at this time as the essential ingredient, kaolin, was known only in China.) By about 1650 the greatly improved technical skills of the potters and the high art of the pottery painters had combined to produce a ware far superior to northern Dutch majolica. Delft ware had assumed its individual character and entered upon its golden age.

Shortly after 1740, however, the pre-eminence of Delft ware yielded to European rivals. In

---

* By 'northern Netherlands' is meant, in contrast to the southern provinces of Flanders, the territory which underwent a series of legal, economic and religious upheavals which began in the reign of Emperor Maximilian of Austria. During the regency of his daughter Margaret they became more acute under Charles V and brought about, under Philip II, the eighty-year war with Spain (1568–1648). The Union of Utrecht (1579) was intended to bring about the unity and independence of the northern provinces, a cause particularly championed by William of Orange. In fact, the union resulted in the establishment of two separate states: the independent Republick der Verenigde zeven Provincies (1648) and the Spanish Netherlands.

1707 the secret of 'true' porcelain was discovered at Meissen in Saxony and Saxon porcelain became common throughout Europe. The new English creamware, evolved by Josiah Wedgwood, was perhaps even more competitively damaging to the Delft industry. Wedgwood's harder ware resisted cracking and the flaking of the glaze far better than the brittle Delft. The economic position of the Delft potters became impossible and shortly after 1800 the Delft potteries had closed. The only exception was De Porceleyne Fles (The Porcelain Bottle) which survived the general decline and after 1876 developed new methods. In this century the N. V. Koninklijke Delftsch-Aardewerk-fabriek De Porceleyne Fles has successfully adapted to international competition.

Ills. 1 a and *1 b. 1 a* (above) shows the 'geeven' or dipping of objects into a tub filled with 'white'. *1 b* shows the 'kwaartton' in which the glaze known as 'kwaart' was applied. (The illustrations are taken from Gerrit Paape's *De Plateelbakker of Delftsch Aardewerk Maaker,* written in 1794.)

I. The Technique

Only one short treatise on the making of Delft faience, *De Plateelbakker of Delftsch Aaarde-werk Maaker* (The Delft Pottery Maker), written by Gerrit Paape in 1794, is now known. It is dedicated to Lambertus Sanderus, the owner of the De Porceleyne Claeuw (The Porcelain Claw) pottery from 1763 to 1805, and it is probable that Paape is writing of techniques which he had come to know in this pottery. His treatise explains the manufacturing technique at a time when the great era of Delft faience had passed, although its production was still considerable. Because of the lack of other studies such as Paape's, it is necessary when studying the history of Delft faience to rely chiefly on research into records such as guild books; baptismal, marriage and death certificates; commercial contracts and, particularly, inventories of Delft faience. This research was begun only about 1900, when there was a revival of interest in Delft. It has already become clear how such research, combined with the scholarly appreciation of the seventeenth and eighteenth-century works of art themselves, has increased our knowledge of Delft pottery.

For the production techniques of northern Dutch majolica our chief sources of information are Italian; it is, after all, in Italy that we find the direct origin of Dutch majolica. The most important source is Cipriano Picolpasso's *Li Tre Libri dell'Arte del Vasaio* (1548). Picolpasso is concerned mainly with the pottery techniques of Urbino, but these are essentially the same as those of other Italian pottery centres, and these are also the techniques which have been most important in Dutch pottery. Early Delft ware is closely similar in many respects to Italian majolica: the differentiation between majolica and Delft faience can be made only in the years following the importation of Chinese porcelain. It was the attempt to imitate this which led to the refining of the Delft material, improved methods of firing, the superiority of its decorations to those of majolica and thus to a distinct 'Delft ware'.

Paape's treatise opens with the statement: 'Delft faience is a certain sort of porcelain invented in the Netherlands about the middle of the last century.' He was, of course, wrong: Delft ware is not porcelain. This mistaken terminology was, as we have seen, common in the seventeenth century and was the subject of a law suit in the Hof van Holland. Paape merely repeats a traditional confusion of terms.

The technique described by Paape has changed remarkably little. According to his treatise, the different kinds of clay were first blended during the washing process which simultaneously purified the material. This washing process produced the 'slip' (clay in solution) which was then cleansed of impurities by filtering. The clean slip settled in a large basin set into the ground and, when the residual water had been drained, was left to dry until it could be cut and placed in a damp cellar. Today, further plasticity and homogeneity are attained in pug-mills; in Paape's day this was achieved by an 'aardetrapper' (literally: clay treader).

The artistic process began with the 'draaier' (literally: wheel-turner) and the 'vormer' (literally: former). All round objects such as bowls and cups were thrown on the potters' wheel by the 'draaier'. When the pieces had dried they were then put on the wheel again for turning. The 'draaier's' art as described by Paape is similar to contemporary techniques. The 'vormer', according to Paape, was responsible for pieces which were not round, or were both round and fluted. These objects were made in specially prepared plaster moulds, as were such objects as spouts and handles. These latter were then attached to the pieces with a thin, very plastic clay called 'kles'. The objects were then thoroughly dried before being fired for the first time. This unglazed fired ware—the 'rauw goed' or 'biscuit'—then underwent a series of further processes such as glazing, decorating and re-firing.

Contemporary methods of glazing are much like the traditional ones described by Paape. The process is as follows: Lead and tin are first melted in the desired proportion and oxydized to tin-ash in a special type of kiln. A compound of sand and salt or sand and soda known as masticot is fired on the floor of the same kiln. A mixture of tin-ash, masticot, salt and soda or potash is then fired to form the 'white'. The 'white' is then pulverized and ground with water until it is very fine. The grinding is done in tubs of water between two stones. As well as the 'white' there is another glaze, called 'kwaart', of similar composition but made without tin and therefore transparent *. Paape reports that in glazing Delft ware the piece was immersed in a tub of 'white' so that it was completely covered, then removed with two fingers of each hand. If necessary the dipping process, called 'geeven', was repeated until the desired thickness of glaze was obtained (*ill. 1 a*).

After these preparations the object was given to the 'plateelschilder' (painter of pottery). Great skill was expected of him and he had special brushes with which he worked. For decorating, the brush was made of the fine hair from the ears of cows, and the painter himself usually made these. (Later, it seems, badger-hair was used.) Brushes known as 'trekkers', with long thin points, were used to draw outlines. 'Sponsen' were also used for outlining. These were cards into which the outline of the design had been pricked. They were pressed against the object and the patterns were then transferred to the glaze by forcing powdered carbon through the very fine holes. The patterns were then traced over with the 'trekker' and the details completed with a coarser brush called a 'dieper'. Many of the pieces, which were already coated with tin glaze, were given a coat of 'kwaart' after painting in order to heighten the gloss. This step, which also prevented the 'white' or the decoration from being damaged or rinsed off, was taken by spraying the piece in a 'kwaartton' or 'kwaart-barrel' (*ill. 1 b*). In the case of majolica the undersides of dishes and the interiors of such objects as apothecary pots were glazed with lead and the surfaces to be painted covered with tin glaze before the painting was begun.

The second firing was decisive for the artistic quality of Delft ware. According to Paape, the

---

* This account is summarized from a catalogue prepared by the Faience Museum in Makkum for an exhibition in 1963.

'plateelbakker' (potter) proved his mastery of his craft at this stage by his technical control of the kiln, the stacking of the pieces and the heating. When the piece was removed from the kiln the 'white' had melted and formed a thick enamel within which the blue or polychrome pattern had been tightly fused.

The kilns themselves have been described by H. W. Mauser. They had several compartments of fire-resistant stone and were about one metre high. Below the compartments was the firebox. Flames and smoke reached the firing chambers through several slits at the bottom and were drawn through a vault into the chimney. A kiln was used at one and the same time for a variety of production phases. Masticot, tin glaze, lead glaze and 'kwaart' were fired at the back of the bottom chamber. New containers (known as 'saggars') for faience were fired in the vault above the firing chamber. The decorated faience was placed in that part of the chamber above the place where the fire was hottest and above it was put the biscuit which was being fired for the first time. All majolica, as well as tiles, were set in the kilns without any protection against smoke and flames but in such a fashion as to prevent damage to the exterior glaze. To avoid individual pieces sticking to one another triangular spurs with a prong at each point known as 'proenen' (*ill. 23*) were inserted between the pieces. Slight marks of the prongs are always visible on such objects.

The finer faience, particularly that which imitated the more delicate Chinese wares, was protected against smoke and flames by means of the ceramic saggars in which it was fired. Here again the individual pieces were kept from fusing by being set on horizontal triangular pegs, or 'struts', let into the walls of the containers. On the backs of the so-called 'pancake' plates of the later period of Delft faience the marks of these pegs may be clearly seen.

Both majolica and Delft faience were fired at temperatures ranging from 900° to 1000° C for seventeen to twenty hours. Between forty and sixty hours were allowed for cooling. Firing at these temperatures presented several difficulties: in the case of gold decoration, and also in that of red, which latter tended to turn brown or to fail to adhere to the tin glaze. These problems were solved by low-temperature firing (at about 600° C) in a specially constructed muffle kiln, a technique adopted about 1700 from that used by the Japanese for Imari porcelain. In this process the ware was particularly well protected—something not always satisfactorily achieved even with the use of containers. Paape does not mention this technique in his treatise, which proves that by his time the muffle kiln was no longer used for faience. It is probable that the De Claeuw potters never even tried this method, although in the middle of the eighteenth century one pottery is known to have used the muffle kiln in imitating Chinese 'famille verte', 'famille rose' and Saxon porcelain.

Let us close this brief description of technique with a note on colouring. The majolica and the tiles of the early period were often polychrome; the preference for blue tiles did not develop until *circa* 1625. Delft faience was predominantly blue in the early period, the reason being the imitation of the Chinese decorations. Polychrome decoration is, however, to be found on the less elaborate ware during the early period and the production of polychrome objects increased toward the end of the seventeenth century when red-and-blue faience was fired at low temperatures in muffle kilns. The peak period of Delft faience—the years between 1670 and 1730—is characterized by both polychrome ware and the excellence of the pieces fired at high temperatures.

II. The Transition from Northern Dutch Majolica to Delft Faience

Owing largely to the research of the Rijksdienst voor het Oudheidkundig Bodemonderzoek (State Institute for Historical Geological Research) we know that between the tenth and the fourteenth centuries three centres in the Netherlands developed the art of making pottery. The products of southern Limburg were distributed, by way of England, to all of north-western Europe. There were also potteries in northern Flanders near Aardenburg, and in the Maas valley, particularly in Andenne, which meant that the northern Netherlands was provided with ceramics for everyday use from three different sources. Until the sixteenth century ceramics were also imported from such places in the lower Rhine valley as Cologne, Frechen, Raeren and Siegburg.

In the history of ceramics in the Netherlands Flanders is much the most important of these centres. In Flanders the import of majolica from Spain, Portugal and Italy, and the adoption of its style by local potters had led, even before 1500, to the creation of an independent 'plateelkunst' (art of pottery). The early Flemish pottery, although made for everyday use, nevertheless displayed artistic merit. These Flemish products were called 'Valensch werck' (Flemish works), majolica being the collective name given to ceramics. Although Flemish tin-glazed ware was known in the area, northern Dutch majolica of this period was still coarse and heavy in material, form and colour, came mainly from Friesland and was exported to northern and western Europe via Hoorn and Enkjuizen. The development of 'plateelbakkerijen' (potteries) in the northern Netherlands was really the result of political and economic events in the south. The fall of Antwerp in 1585, a consequence of the revolt of the Netherlands against Spain, led to a large-scale migration north. Among those who fled were potters who undoubtedly stimulated the development, improvement and refinement of northern Dutch majolica, particularly in Haarlem, Amsterdam, Gouda, Rotterdam and Delft. The provenance of individual pieces of this peroid cannot be established on the basis of style or pattern as the painters copied each other's designs. Typical decorations of the time were: colourful bowls with a pomegranate pattern which, about 1600, was also to be found on tiles; plates with a geometrical pattern, not to be found on tiles; plates with the blue-and-white leaf pattern of northern Italian origin, as well as numerous variations and combinations of these motifs.

The border decoration of the plates is similarly unconfined to one pattern. Its evolution cannot be chronologically catalogued, although it may be surmised that the simple cross-hatching or linear border decoration is the oldest design used in the northern Netherlands. There were also

Ill. 2. Fragment of a polychrome majolica plate. Found in a canal in Delft. Virgin with the Christ child. Manufactured before 1600 in Delft (?). Amsterdam, Rijksmuseum.

Ill. 3. Polychrome majolica plate with blue Wan Li border. Virgin with the Christ child, surrounded by an aureole. First part of the 17th century. Northern Netherlands. Rotterdam, Boymans van Beuningen Museum.

Ill. 4. Polychrome majolica plate with blue Wan Li border. The inscription in the cartouche, which is formed by figures, reads: 'Eedt niet sonder Got te eeren' (Do not eat without honouring God). About 1625. Northern Netherlands (?). The Hague, Gemeente Museum.

Ill. 5. Blue majolica bowl with Chinese decoration. 1600–1625. Northern Netherlands, Delft (?). Rotterdam, Boymans van Beuningen Museum.

Plate I
Small blue majolica bowl for mash or purée with
Chinese decoration and Wan Li border. 1600–25.
Northern Netherlands, Delft (?). Rotterdam, Boy-
mans van Beuringen Museum.

Plate II
Blue majolica plate with Chinese decoration and
Wan Li border; *c.* 1625. Utrecht, Central Museum.

Ill. 6. Polychrome majolica bowl with Wan Li decoration and geometrical border ornamentation. On the back, the letters A. F. After 1650. Frisian faience from Makkum. Makkum, Museum 'De Waag'.

scalloped, bossed borders, and lozenge motifs, probably of Frisian origin. Shortly after 1600 a Far Eastern element was added for the first time to European majolica by the adoption of some of the Chinese Wan Li blue-and-white religious symbols as border decoration and the imitation of Chinese figures, landscapes and flowers.

A brief historical note is necessary here. The Dutch, who travelled to China for the first time in 1596, came upon porcelain 'more exquisite than crystal' as the navigator Jan Huygen van Linschoten (1563–1611) described it in his *Navigatio ac itinerarium*. In 1602 Chinese porcelain was imported into the northern Netherlands for the first time in any quantity and was auctioned in Middelburg. The Dutch East India Company was formed in the same year by the Netherlands states-general and it was the import agent for Chinese porcelain until 1795. The company combined existing and competitive separate companies in the Far East into a single organization, intended to discharge governmental functions, prosecute the war with the Spanish and the Portuguese and regulate trade. The new company was capitalized by national subscription and the independence of states comprising the United Netherlands was recognized by the creation of local boards at Delft, Amsterdam and elsewhere which directed the trade of their own districts. The real governing authority of the company was the 'collegium' of seventeen members, sixteen of whom were chosen from the general directorate in proportion to the share which each local branch had contributed to the capital or joint stock. Delft, which had subscribed an eighth, was represented by two members. (The seventeenth member was nominated in succession by other members of the United Netherlands.) The headquarters of the company were fixed at Batavia,

while a committee of ten in The Hague transacted the company's business with the states-general. In 1624 Zeelandia, on Formosa, became the porcelain depot from which all export agents in east Asia, with the exception of those in Batavia, provided the Netherlands with porcelain, and the Netherlands in turn dominated the European porcelain market.

A porcelain auction took place in Delft in 1615 and this was probably the moment in time when the basis for Delft faience was laid. The import of great quantities of Chinese porcelain had begun during the reign of the Ming Emperor Wan Li (1573—1619) and the Wan Li designs were copied by the Delft potters. At first these imitations of the Wan Li border with the characteristic symbols were awkwardly done, but gradually the Delft design became more sophisticated as the border and the central motif of the piece were related more closely to each other.

Among the earliest northern Netherlands majolica were plates representing the Virgin holding the Christ child, the heads surrounded by aureoles with simple lines leading to the borders of the plates, an example of which is shown in *illustration 2*, a fragment of a polychrome plate found in a canal in Delft and probably locally made. Blue and polychrome plates were manufactured well into the seventeenth century. Some, with Wan Li borders, depicted the Virgin and Child (*ill. 3*) and a number bore edifying sayings such 'Eert Godt Altyt' (Honour God at all times) or 'Eedt Niet sonder Godt te Eeren' (Do not eat without honouring God) and also had Wan Li borders (*ill. 4*). The latter, a particularly beautiful example of its type, may

Ill. 8. Fragment of an apothecary jar showing a cartouche and city gates. About 1600–1625. Northern Netherlands. Hoorn, Westfries Museum.

have been designed and made by a Flemish painter in the Netherlands. A small bowl for mash or *purée* (Plate I) and a decorative plate of similar style (*ill. 5*) are particularly characteristic of the ware dating from the early period of Delft faience. They suggest a Flemish potter working in Delft, since the bowl, which copies the shape of small tin equivalents, is of a type commonly used in the southern Netherlands but which almost never occurred in the north. The blue plate (Plate II) decorated with Chinese plants and a border of symbols is an early, rare example which demonstrates that the unity of Chinese composition had been achieved by the Dutch. A variation of the design, a colourful geometrical lozenge pattern on the border, is of Frisian origin and proves that the Chinese porcelain patterns spread throughout the Netherlands (*ill. 6*).

Finally a few remarks about pots for salves, pill vases, apothecary jars or 'albarelli', and syrup jugs which originated in Flanders or the Netherlands. The decoration of the first two groups is limited to polychrome lines, braided designs on the border and zig-zag motifs. After 1630 these designs were replaced by a cartouche, richly decorated with Flemish-Italian Renaissance motifs (putti, fleur-de-lis, garlands, peacocks etc.), which was used to label the contents. Again, these were blue on a white background. About the year 1650 they were mainly manufactured in Delft, although Haarlem was also known for them. The shape of the large apothecary jars is reminiscent of a segment of bamboo cane. It is almost impossible to determine whether they are of Flemish or Dutch origin, although it is known that jars with the leaf pattern (*ill. 7*), were manufactured in Rotterdam. It is however possible to assign an approximate date to them. The oldest examples are lead-glazed on the interior and tin-glazed on the exterior; it was not until the seventeenth century that exclusive use of the tin glaze was made. The closing also reveals a good deal: a rim with a lip permits us to assume a parchment or pig's bladder covering, a smooth rim indicates a copper lid while a threaded rim dates from a later period.

A very rare piece from the nothern Netherlands is an apothecary jar with a cartouche on one side, while on the other there is a view of a harbour and two figures looking out over the harbour wall (*ill. 8*). This jar was excavated in Hoorn but was probably made in Haarlem or Amsterdam.

III. Tiles and Plaques: 1600—1700. Frederik van Frijtom

Some consideration of the northern Dutch tile industry is necessary for a full understanding of Delft ceramics. Technically the tiles differ from majolica because of the coarser composition of the basic material. The thickness of the early tiles varied from 18 to 20 mm. It was not until the seventeenth century that potters successfully manufactured tiles which were between 11 and 13 mm. thick and which on average were 13 cm. square. Usually the tiles were not 'gekwaart' (*i.e.,* double-glazed, with clear lead over-glaze on the tin glaze). Nor were they protected against smoke and flames in the kilns. They were set upright in the kilns, separated by two thin clay rolls and were covered by a row which had been fired once and which were laid flat. Thousands of tiles could thus be fired simultaneously. A practical method for applying the decorations was also developed for this mass production. The technique of using 'sponsen' made it possible to apply circles, flourishes and figures, in short, the whole pattern. The outlines were then painted over with a brush and shaded.

Originally Rotterdam, Delft, Haarlem, Amsterdam, Gouda and Utrecht were the centres of tile manufacture but soon the production spread to the northern Netherlands and Friesland so that a national industry developed. Certain factories were always the property of one family, for example the Tichelaar Royal Faience and Tile factory in Makkum. The factories often worked closely together and, as archives show, even exchanged personnel and designs. It is thus rarely possible to determine the place of origin of a tile.

The tiles can however be classified distinctly according to manner and style. The oldest 'Antwerp' style shows the Hispano-Moresque influence. White is reserved in a four-colour geometrical pattern; a hexagonal or octagonal star with half or quarter circles in braided lines results in a design formed by the four corner patterns which can be repeated continuosly (*ill. 9*). This basic integrated pattern was continued for a long time in a number of variations. However, when Dutch tile art developed its own style at the beginning of the seventeenth century, the corner pattern resulting from the four-tile unit no longer represented anything but a simple rosette or flower unrelated to the central motif (*ills. 20, 21*). Other decorative patterns consisted of fleurs-de lis (*ills. 11* and *14*), arabesques, called in the trade 'ossekoppen', *i.e.* oxen heads, (*ill. 12*), or the maze design which formed a harmonious whole together with a flowing octagonal curve around a Chinese flower vase motif (*ill. 10*).

About the year 1600, the pomegranate pattern combined with grapes and marigolds executed in orange, yellow, blue and green was very popular. An inventory drawn up in 1603 calls them 'orange

Ill. 9. Polychrome tile with Hispano-Mooresque motifs. The corner design is reserved in white. Delft, Rijksmuseum Huis Lambert van Meerten.

Ill. 10. Blue tile with Chinese flower vase and fretted or Wan Li corner design. Rotterdam, Boymans van Beuningen Museum.

apples'. These tiles, in units of four, can also form an infinitely repeating pattern (*ill. 11*). 'Orange apples' and grapes artfully arranged on a Renaissance dish are a variation on this theme (*ill. 12*). Quite unique are the fairly rare tiles decorated with small winged cherub heads surrounded by a wreath of vines and shaded in blue and white, a motif used earlier as ornamentation for majolica (*ill. 13, cf.* also *ill. 7*). After that, Dutch tile production of local inspiration enjoyed a period of great popularity. The tiles in question were polychrome flower tiles copied from engravings of artificially cultivated 'Europeesche en overzeesche Gewassen' as shown in the *Florilegia* or the *Hortus Floridus* by Crispijn van de Passe (called *Den Blomhof* in the Dutch translation, 1614). Many of the tulip books by Dutch flower painters were illustrated in a similar manner about 1650 (*ills. 14, 15*).

Also among the pieces dating from the early seventeenth century which are of great artistic value are the tiles depicting soldiers. They owe much to the style of the engravings of Jacob de Gheyn. Polychrome tiles showing soldiers carrying pikes or muskets are a good example of this type of tile (*ills. 20, 21*). The best of them by far are in Beauregard castle in the series based on Prince Maurice's famous book *Wapehnhandelinghe van Roers, Musquetten en Spiessen* (The Making of Firelocks, Muskets and Pikes) which was published in Amsterdam in 1607 and between 1608 and 1720 appeared in French, English, German and Danish editions. These tiles must have been made in Rotterdam or Delft, since the archives of Beauregard castle near Blois indicate that sixteen crates, containing more than 7,000 tiles, were sent (from Delftshaven?) to Nantes and from there via Blois to

Ill. 11. Four polychrome tiles with pomegranates and grapes, fleur-de-lis corner design. Rotterdam, Historisch Museum.

Beauregard castle. The shipment was paid for on December 12, 1627. The floor, which is still called 'toute une armée en marche' was not, however, laid until 1646 (*ills. 16—19*).

Meanwhile a pronounced preference for blue tiles developed. Since the tile industry had spread throughout the whole country the choice of decorative motifs was practically unlimited. Besides soldiers, burghers in fashionable dress or practising their professions were represented, as well as animals, birds, landscapes, river views with houses, bridges and fishermen, city vistas, ships and even children playing. Biblical scenes were also depicted. Tiles by the thousands, with an enormous variety of designs, were sold internationally.

Dutch tiles were mainly used to decorate the interiors of houses, although on occasion they were also used for ornamenting the gables. In the entrance hall, passageways and staircases, tiles were used as panelling and decoration to the height of one metre in order to protect clothing against the whitewashed walls. Proverbial Dutch cleanliness soon introduced tiling into the kitchen, and somewhat later rooms of the Baroque period were provided with a tile border above the marble floor so that the wall would not be damaged when the floor was scrubbed. About 1630, the bricks on both sides of the iron hearthplate of the fireplaces were replaced by blue tiles; the 'schoorsteen-pilaertjes' (imitations of marble pillars which appeared on mantlepieces) were fashionable in the Baroque period. In the eighteenth century tiles were made with a violet or manganese background while the design was usually blue. Entire rooms were tiled with blue or manganese pictures framed by white tiles.

Ill. 12. Polychrome tiles with Renaissance fruit dish, filled with pomegranates and grapes. Arabesque corner design. Delft, Rijksmuseum Huis Lambert van Meerten.

Meanwhile, about 1700, exports increased to an unprecedented extent. As the Hispano-Portuguese tile industry began to decline, Dutch tiles began to replace it. They were supplied by the thousands for Catholic churches, convents and cloisters. Dutch tiles can even be found in South America as J. M. Dos Santos Simoês of Lisbon has shown. During the same period it became fashionable to tile whole rooms and staircases in European baroque castles (among others Rambouillet, Nymphenburg near Munich, Niëborov near Warsaw, now the Institute for Art History).

Around 1900, an interest in tiles and in Delft faience developed. Tiles from demolished houses and farms were put on the market as antiques and were used for the open fireplaces ('Hollandse Schouw') in the houses of the wealthy. However, the intimate atmosphere of seventeenth-century rooms, as shown in the paintings of the 'Golden Age', was never achieved. The use of antique tiles in modern buildings therefore remained a passing fancy.

Historical research has established that Rotterdam always had the largest number of tile factories. After the Twelve-Year Truce of 1609 with Spain, the industry throughout the country expanded considerably. Only ten of the nearly eighty tile factories were located in Delft. It was therefore incorrect, when renewed attention was given to Delft after 1900, to speak of 'Delft' tiles as if Delft had been a leading producer in this industry. All we can determine from inventories is that before 1620, Paulus Bourseth's Rouaen factory manufactured a fairly large number of tiles, while De Twee Scheepjes (The Two Little Ships) a factory in which Aelbrecht Keyzer worked and of which he became owner in 1642, underwent alterations so as to permit the production of tiles with a tin glaze. In Delft the transition had already been made to the firing of 'porceleyn', as the finer Delft ware was called, and the industry was mainly geared to producing this.

One artist of the Dutch tile industry deserves particular mention: Frederik van Frijtom. Being an independent master potter and pottery painter and, above all, a landscape painter, he possessed all the qualities necessary to give an individual character to faience and to represent the Dutch polder landscape in an unequalled manner. He chose for this purpose small plaques and round plates between 22 and 25 cm. in diameter, on which he only filled the centre space, leaving the border without decoration. He did not use 'sponsen'; he himself made the sketch and then, with perfect control over his brush, drew, shaded and stippled and thus managed to capture the atmosphere of a landscape. He created perspective by using different shades of blue and represented clouds by using gradations ranging from blue to white, an effect which is characteristic of his art. We know dated

Plate III
Small plaque with a river view of the village of
Overschie. Signed: F. v. Frijtom 1692. Private
collection.

Ill. 13. Four blue tiles with cherub heads and leaf ornament. Delft, Rijksmuseum Huis Lambert van Meerten.

Ill. 14. Polychrome tile with a flower copied from the *Florilegia.* Fleur-de-lis corner design. Rotterdam, Historisch Museum.

and signed plaques of the years 1659 and 1692 (*ill. 22* and Plate III). The latter represents a view of the village of Overschie. With it he broke away from imaginary Italian landscapes and developed his own vision of the misty Dutch riverscape which is the high point of his art.

In 1658 he was listed in the Delft citizens' register as 'Komende van buyten' (coming from abroad). He worked independently and was not a member of the Guild of St Luke. His wife's will referred to him as 'gildeknecht' (guildsman). He died shortly before 1702. He willed to his wife 'twee steen gebacken schilde rijtjes' (two paintings fired on stone), which are still listed in her inventory in 1710 as 'twee aerde schilderijen met houten lijsten' (two earthenware paintings in

Ills. 16—19. Four blue tiles: a halberdier, a musketeer, a trumpeter on horseback and a horseman in armour, framed by octagonal curves with leaf patterns in the corners. The first two are copied from engravings by Jakob de Gheyn. All four still form part of the tiled floor of the great hall of Beauregard Castle near Blois.

Ills. 20, 21. Two polychrome tiles depicting soldiers. They are copied from engravings by Jakob de Gheyn. Rosette corner design, white leaves on a blue background. Delft, Rijksmuseum Huis Lambert van Meerten.

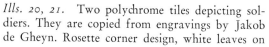

Ill. 22. Large blue plaque depicting in Italian landscape. Signed: F. v. Frijtom 1659. Amsterdam, Rijksmuseum.

28

wooden frames). Lambert Cleffius of De Metalen Pot (The Metal Pot) also owned in 1691 'een porceleyn lantschap door Frijtom' (a porcelain landscape by Frijtom). Altogether about forty of his works have been preserved, mainly landscapes on plaques or plates. One of the exceptions is a wine jug mounted in silver, one of his finest pieces. The decoration shows a boar hunt in a forest which is hazily depicted in the distance, another characteristic of Frijtom's technique (*ills. 24, 25*).

Frijtom's great artistry was never matched again although other artists continued to paint lands-cape plaques. We know Italian landscapes dating from the same period which Dutch painters portrayed upon returning from study trips to Italy. There are, for example, two plaques dating from the year 1659, for which an unknown painter based himself on the etchings of Nicolaas Brechem (Plate IV). By comparison Frijtom's talent is particulary striking.

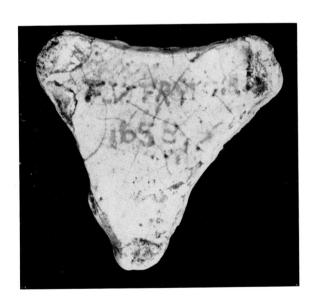

Ill. 23. 'Proen'. Flat triangular slab with a prong at each corner. Signed: F. v. Frijtom 1658. Private collection.

Ills. 24, 25. Wine jug with handle, mounted in silver. The ornamentation represents a boar hunt. End of 17th century. Private collection.

IV. 'Wapengoet en Porceleyn'—'Kaapsche Schotels'.
Delft Faience 1650—1700

When, shortly before 1650, the pottery factories in Delft developed their own decorative style the foundation was laid for Delft faience — a ware unique of its kind which had a brilliant future before it. By contrast, elsewhere in the Netherlands the quality of majolica never surpassed the standard which had been reached by the middle of the seventeenth century.

In 1654 Delft was almost completely destroyed by the explosion of a boat loaded with gunpowder. A large quantity of early Delft faience must have been lost in the blast. The reconstruction of the city took many years, during which unused breweries, whose export trade had declined, were converted into potteries. Frequently the potteries retained the names of the breweries, such as 'The

Ill. 26. Urbino bowl with yellow, brown and violet grotesque ornament. Probably from the northern Netherlands. Middle of the 17th century. Rotterdam, Boymans van Beuningen Museum.

Plate IV
Small plaque showing cattle and a herdsman in an
Italian landscape. It was probably inspired by a
print by Nicolaas Berchem. Second part of the 17th
century. Unsigned. Private collection.

Plate V
Octagonal plate with broad border. At the centre,
an inscription framed by Renaissance motifs and a
crown. Delft (?), end of the 17th century. Privately
owned.

Plate VI
Plaque with a portrait of Dionysius Spranckhuysen, pastor in Delft, copied from an engraving by Crispijn van den Queborn (from 1641–60). Delft, no mark, about 1650. Amsterdam, Rijksmuseum.

Plate VII
Two small blue candlesticks with Chinese decoration. Mark: D with a shaft and the number 24. De Dissel, about 1660. The Hague, Gemeente Museum.

Plate VIII
Small jar with three medallions and Chinese figures.
Mark: IW (Jakob Wemmerson Hoppesteyn). Het
Jonge Moriaenshooft, before 1670. Arnhem, Gem-
eente Museum.

Plate IX

One of two water bottles decorated with scenes
from Greek mythology. Apollo here pursues Daphne who is turned into a tree. On the reverse side
Leukippos is repulsed by Daphne and Apollo
rides through the air on his chariot. (The second
water bottle depicts Orpheus followed by a woman,
perhaps Eurydice. On its reverse Orpheus is recognized by the Maenads, the votaries of Dionysus,
and is killed by them.) De Grieksche A, 1686–1701.
Arnhem, Gemeente Museum.

Three Golden Ash-Barrels', 'The Four Roman Heroes' and 'The Double Jug'. A word is needed here concerning the administration of the potteries in order to make clear who the artists producing Delft ceramics really were. The potteries were business enterprises which the city administration encouraged and supported. The management of the potteries however was seldom in the hands of the potters and painters themselves who did not have sufficient capital; rather it was usually taken on by wealthy citizens of Delft who considered the potteries a good investment. But according to the regulations of the Guild of St Luke into which the craft workers were organized, no one who was not himself a master potter or painter of pots could manage a factory. This regulation, however, could easily be circumvented by appointing a member of the guild as 'shopkeeper' or manager a procedure by which the actual owner was 'released' as it was termed. The manager became, in effect, the director of the pottery, often in collaboration with others; sometimes he also became a co-owner.

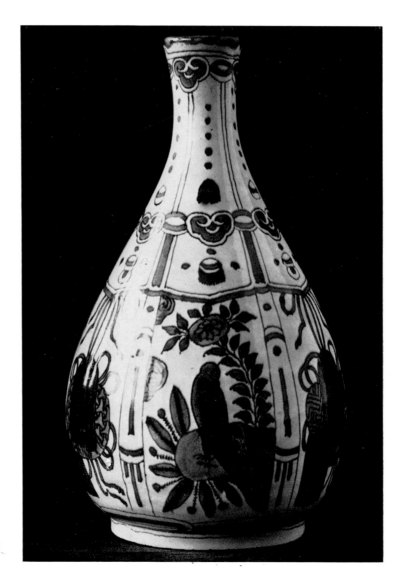

Ill. 27. Bottle with Wan Li decoration. Delft, about 1670. The Hague, Gemeente Museum.

Ill. 28. Large plate representing Christ and the woman taken in adultery. Delft, no mark, 1651. Privately owned.

To give an example: the name Van Eenhorn is inseparably connected with the development of Delft faience in the middle of the seventeenth century and continued to be so, through various marriages, until about 1773. Wouter van Eenhorn (d. 1679) is particulary important. He was the founder, owner or co-owner of no less than five potteries and did business with the town of Harlingen in Friesland, with Utrecht, London and Paris. In 1655 he and Quirinus van Cleynhoven bought De Porceleyne Fles. It would seem that at that time he was not a potter for there is a clause to the effect that Quirinus van Cleynhoven was to be 'shopkeeper' and to instruct Van Eenhoorn in everything to do with the art of pottery. He must have become a very able potter, judging by the business he did, and in 1667 the magistrats of Delft bought from him a number of vases costing '378 gulden en 10 stuyvers' as a wedding present for the Swedish ambassador, Count Dohna. In 1658 he bought the brewery De Grieksche A (The Greek A) and became 'shopkeeper' so that he must have been a master potter by this time although we do not know any of his works. Between 1663 and 1678 he was its sole owner although his son Samuel took over the management in 1674. Wouter was also at various times co-owner of De 3 Vergulde Astonnekens (The Three Golden Ash-Barrels), Het Hooge Huys (The High House) and De Paeuw (The Peacock). His importance to Delft pottery is indisputable, not least with respect to its finances and in particular those of De Grieksche A.

Discussion of the owners and managers of potteries inevitably leads to the question of the marks which appear on Delft ware. A word of caution is necessary here, however: unmarked pieces must not be neglected, for this category includes many works of art of the highest quality. It is the quality of the individual piece which must be of first consideration in evaluating any work of Delft art. There are, none the less, sufficient very good reasons for continuing historical research into records and archives. The more that is learned about the origin, the dating, the decoration and the style of Delft faience, the sooner we will be able to arrive at a proper appreciation of this form of art.

The crux of the problem of marks is what significance should be attached to them. Do they indicate artistic achievement or are they merely of historical importance? In the case of initials which are used as marks it is necessary to ascertain whether they stand for the name of the owner of the pottery or whether they designate an artist, either a master potter or a painter. Research into records has shown that in the case of several groups of initials both the name of the owner of the pottery and that of an artist are indicated. Nevertheless, in most cases only the name of the pottery itself is indicated. Indeed, there is rarely any information available about the artists other than their names. Frederik van Frijtom is an exception, but he of course worked independently.

The years 1650—1700 were decisive in the attainment of higher artistic standards. The pieces known at the time as 'Wapengoet en Porceleyn' (earthenware with heraldic decorations) are examples of the new excellence. (Other examples are the ware known as 'Wit Goet'—white earthenware—and 'Straets Goet', i.e., imitations made in Delft of pieces imported from Italy via the Strait of Gibraltar.) Plates V—VII illustrate the high qualitiy of objects produced in these years.

So-called 'porceleyn' in the Wan Li style continued to develop during these years. A bottle-shaped vase ornamented with birds, flowers and Chinese symbols shows a much greater and more tasteful understanding of the design, colouration and glazed hues of Ming porcelain (ill. 27).

Ill. 29. Blue bowl with Chinese decoration. Mark: CK with a shaft and the number 34 (Cornelis van der Kloot). De Dissel, 1694—97. Leeuwarden, Museum Het Princessehof.

Ill. 30. 'Kaapsche Schotel' with Chinese decoration. Mark: LVE (Lambert van Eenhoorn). De Metalen Pot, 1691–1721. Privately owned.

In the southern Netherlands potteries imitated Italian Renaissance ceramics. We may cite as examples the bowls made in the style of the Patanazzi workshop in Urbino: large ceremonial bowls with broad borders and yellow-brown grotesque ornaments with purple outlines which were probably manufactured only in Antwerp. In the northern Netherlands this style was used only sporadically; one example is a blue bowl dated 1661 on which a medallion frames a portrait of Prince William III in his youth.

Smaller, deep Urbino bowls were imported in large quantities. Imitations of these made in the Netherlands are often practically identical with the imports. The bowl shown in *illustration 26* may have been made in the northern Netherlands, possibly in Rotterdam or Delft, as the border with the simple hatching suggests.

Delft faience was certainly influenced by the Urbino bowls. This is true particularly for 'wit goet' (white ware without decoration), the term applied to all tableware and household objects such as pitchers, bowls with fluted rims and plates in various shapes whose sober magnificence is to be found depicted in the still-life paintings of the period. Related to these objects are the 'sunflower' bowls (*ill. 33*). At the time of the Stadtholder, William III of England (reigned 1689–1702) and Queen Mary (d. 1694) these bowls were ornamented with a portrait of the sovereigns and a border of sunflowers, tulips and orange-fruit. Plates of this type were also made by Dutchmen in Lambeth, London. There are various styles of the so-called Lambeth-Delft faience, but it can normally be distinguished from the genuine Delft.

The reputation of Delft faience was established for all time because of the wealth of its decorative

36

themes which were taken from Dutch painting and graphic arts. Riverscapes or sea-side land-scapes, portraits, interiors, scenes from rural life and other motifs were represented on plaques framed in black which replaced paintings on walls.

Coats of arms ('wapengoet'), particularly those of cities, were used to decorate majolica as early as 1610 but this style of ornamentation became more common about 1650 when family, as well as imaginary, coats of arms became fashionable. Haarlem was especially noted for this type of ware but plates with the coats of arms of Delft families, some executed very much in the style of Van Bleyswijk, are known from at least 1662. Monogrammed plates were introduced for families which did not have coats of arms; the monograms were circumscribed, like a coat of arms, by an elegant Renaissance motif with a crown. We know examples dating form the years 1691 and 1701. At the bottom of a soup bowl (privately owned in England) the same motif is found, with the mark 'Z. E. 1686'. It is probably Lambeth ware.

Another period style of interest is that of plates inscribed with Dutch rhymes. Each plate was numbered from 1 to 6 and on each was inscribed one line of a couplet, the three couplets comprising a verse. Each line was circumscribed with an ornate design containing a crown (Plate V). Three such series of couplets are known. Some of these were translated into English and the poor spelling of the translation leads one to suppose that these dishes were manufactured in Lambeth by artists from Delft. This type of inscribed plate was also adopted in England and several series of English couplets are known. The most famous is the 'merryman' series and inscribed English plates are known

Ill. 31. 'Kaapsche Schotel' with Chinese decoration. Mark L. C. (Lambert Cleffius). De Metalen Pot, 1670–1691. Arnhem, Gemeente Museum.

generically as 'merryman' plates. (See Anthony Ray, *English Delftware Pottery in the Robert Hall Warren Collection*, Faber, London 1968, page 145 and plate 17.)

Representations of Biblical scenes appealed greatly to the piety of the overwhelmingly Protestant Netherlands. Dutch graphic art inspired a bowl, dated 1651 (*ill. 28*), representing Christ and the woman taken in adultery. An inscription along the rim reads 'Dit is het vroutge dat in overspel warde bevonden en war beclaecht. Vnd. 10 en. Anno 1651' (This is the woman who was caught in adultery and accused. . . .Tenth month of the year 1651). In the lower lefthand side Christ writes on the stone floor 'Die sonder sonden is die werpt . . .' (Let he who is without sin cast . . .). The bowl, and another dated 1650, is of heavy red clay, coated with white glaze and painted in deep blue.

Several ceramic-portraits of personalities famous in the sciences, theology and history are of high quality. All of them are copied from etchings by Crispijn van den Queborn (1604–54). Among them is the plaque with the portrait of Dionysius Spranckhuysen, a Delft preacher (Plate VI). The mausoleum of Prince William of Orange, constructed by Hendrik de Keyser in 1620, was reproduced on a plaque dated May 10, 1657 and signed by Isaack Junius (*ill. 32*). The 'nieuwe inventien' stimulated the extension of the potteries and the number of master potters and painters steadily increased. It is to them that we owe the development of faience from Delft earthenware.

At first this development was as anonymous as that of majolica. The rôle played by the artists themselves—the men who actually designed and decorated the ceramics—remains unknown. In the later stages of the development of Delft, however, a closer collaboration arose among the factory owners, the managers, and the artists who planned and the craftsmen who executed a project. This collaboration makes it frequently possible to determine the origin of works of Delft art, and it is a collaboration which is important both in the history of the development of the art itself and because it enables us to discover this history.

De Dissel (The Pole)

Thanks to the research of Dr H. E. van Gelder we can use this pottery as an example of the development of Delft potteries. So much material is to be found in the records of the period that we can draw a picture of De Dissel which, although not altogether complete, is based entirely on historical documents. It is possible here, however, to give only a very shortened account of this history.

The De Dissel mark comprises a thistle and the letter D and in the years 1666–94, there is usually a date. In the years 1694–97 the marks sometimes incorporate the initials CK, standing for Cornelius van der Kloot who had been a painter at the pottery since 1671.

The Cruyck family owned De Dissel in the years 1640–66; no marks are known from that period. Abraham de Cooge, an art dealer, was the pottery's sole owner until 1682 when a Leendert Boersse became owner. The business met with financial difficulties, yearly receipts dropping from about 25,000 guilders to 11,000 guilders. In 1694 Adriaen Kocks, the owner of De Griecksche A, bought 'de geabandonneerde boedel' (the abandoned property) for 2,300 guilders. Cornelius van der Kloot remained in the business as painter and Pieter van den Hurck, a master potter, became manager. In 1701 De Griecksche A took over all the remaining stock and Pieter van den Hurck also went over to

Ill. 32. Small plaque representing the mausoleum of Prince William of Orange in the Alten
Kirche in Delft, copied from an
engraving by Isaac Junius. Delft,
no mark, 1657. Delft, Museum
Het Prinsenhof.

it. In the same year the factory was sold to Jacobus de Caluwe, 'meester theepotjesbacker' (master
teapot maker) who manufactured red teapots (see page 68) until some time after 1711. The building
later reverted to its original use as a brewery.

A relatively large number of pieces with the motif of a grasshopper sitting on a rock surrounded by
bushes are to be found among blue Delft. Van der Kloot was using this pattern in 1695. He also
designed plant motifs which surround, like an aureole, a small central medaillon (*ill. 29*).

There also exist polychrome Delft barber's bowls and numerous plates depicting flowering plants,
made well into the eighteenth century, which have the complete De Dissel mark on them (see
marks 27—32). It can therefore be assumed with near certainty that in 1701 De Grieksche A took
over all the designs of the factory and thereafter continued to use the De Dissel mark.

'Kaapsche Schotels' (Plates from the Cape)

About 1675 a special type of Delft faience developed which came to be known as 'Kaapsche Scho-tels'. These were imitations of imports from China of specially designed ceremonial plates for which the expression 'porceleyn-karakter' (porcelain-character) is particulary apt. These plates are in the Wan Li style but they are outstanding for the delicacy of their decoration and execution. The large polygonal medallion contains a landscape with a background of luxuriant plants and in the foreground a single bird, a pelican or a peacock spreading his tale, or a solitary stag. Sometimes one also finds a roll of papyrus on a step or a flowerpot filled with chrysanthemums on a pedestal. To match the polygon in the centre, the Wan Li symbols are repeated along the border where they alternate with Chinese symbols which are drawn within small frames. The colour is dark blue verging on violet which heightens their decorative effectiveness. A technical refinement was acheived at the same time by the use of the 'trek'—outlining in black or dark blue—a technique which was probably invented by Samuel van Eenhorn and which was used from then on in decorating Delft faience. Paape refers to this technique in his 1794 treatise. He talks of 'the paint with which painters traced the outlines of their paintings in order to set them off more distinctly against the blue'. For this purpose, he says, 'Sapphire-blue or rust-red can be used . . . Otherwise one can use "dirty blue", which is blue collected from the jugs in which the brushes are cleaned. This is then used with sapphire and with it a clear outline may be made.'

Many of the 'Kaapsche Schotels' bear the mark of, and consequently originate from, De Metalen Pot (The Metal Pot) at the time of Lambert Cleffius (1661—91) or Lambert van Eenhoorn (1691 —1721). *Illustrations 30* and *31* show examples of their work. Other works of this genre originated from Het Jonge Moriaenshooft (The Young Moor's Head) and De Porceleyne Fles.

Ill. 33. Small white bowl with gadrooned rim. Polychrome bird and tulip decoration. Delft, second half of the 17th century. The Hague, Gemeente Museum.

V. Blue Delft: 1670—1730

Wan Li—whose name was given to a style of porcelain decoration—reigned as emperor of China from 1572 to 1620. He was a member of the Ming dynasty which was overthrown in 1644 and succeeded by the Ch'ing dynasty. During the revolution the Chinese porcelain industry suffered severely when a number of factories were destroyed, but none the less it was under the Ch'ings that the vogue for Chinese porcelain reached its greatest heights in Europe. The Chinese industry flourished particularly under Emporer K'ang-hsi (1661—1722), a notable patron of the arts, and his two successors. K'ang-hsi gave considerable support to the director of the imperial kilns of Ching-tê Chên and the Dutch East India Company sold this porcelain throughout Europe.

The Wan Li style of design had first been used in the Netherlands by the De Dissel pottery. With the K'ang-hsi style a wealth of new motifs was introduced and its influence upon blue Delft faience is apparent. It can be seen, for example, in the more delicate representation of female figures and of dancing children, the so-called 'zotjes' ('sillies'); in the depiction of different flora and fauna, and in the design with 'Franse-punt' (French-point) which filled the whole border and which is to be found both in blue on a white background and in white on blue. These elegant decorations were executed in dark blue and covered with a brilliant glaze.

Het Jonge Moriaenshooft (The Young Moor's Head) *1660—92*

The reputation of this factory was established by Jacob Wemmerson Hoppesteyn and his son Rochus. Jacob became a master potter in 1660 and from 1664 until his death in 1671 he was the sole owner of this factory. (From 1657—68 he was also co-owner of De Porceleyne Bijl (The Porcelain Axe) but we know nothing of what influence he had on this factory nor of any work which can be attributed to him.) In the year of his death Jacob also became 'shopkeeper' of Het Jonge Moriaenshooft. Jacob's widow remarried Willem van Teylingen and she and her new husband managed the factory until his death in 1679. From then until her own death in 1686 she and her son Rochus, who had obtained his master-craftsman's certificate in 1680 when he was only nineteen, were the managers. Rochus became sole owner on his mother's death and remained so until he died in 1692 in which year it was sold to Lieven van Dalen.

The contribution of the Hoppesteyns' is of great importance in the development of decorative pottery. We have no records as to what extent Jacob was personally involved in the making

Ill. 34. Large vase with two handles. Chinese plant decoration with peacocks. Mark: IW (Jacob Wemmerson Hoppesteyn). Het Jonge Moriaenshooft, before 1670. Amsterdam, Rijksmuseum.

of pottery in his early career, but Rochus we know to have been a superb craftsman and his works represent the highest achievement in the manufacture of polychrome Delft faience (see Chapter VII).

The numerous works which have come down to us with the monogram IW, *i.e.,* Jacob Wemmerson (Mark 91; *ills. 34, 35;* Plate VIII), represent striking scenes from Greek mythology, such as the labours of Hercules or the story of Niobe; and from Church history, for example, the lives of the apostles. They also depict mountain landscapes based on Italian originals. He was, of course, also influenced by Chinese porcelain. The great variety of themes leads to the conclusion that there were several 'plateelschilders', whose names remain unknown, working in the pottery. Indeed we do not know whether Jacob Wemmerson himself was one of the artists. In this connection, one detail deserves particular attention, namely the so-called 'Hoppensteyn—borders'. To judge from their style they date from the last years of the Ming dynasty or the first of the Ch'ing. They exist in blue as well as in a polychrome combination of violet, blue, green, bright red or with a golden sheen. Possibly these borders establish a link with the work of Rochus Hoppensteyn. In any case, from a technical point of view, they are the most important objects produced by Het Jonge Moriaenshooft.

De Grieksche A (The Greek A) *1674–1722*

Samuel, the youngest son of Wouter van Eenhoorn (d. 1679), the founder of this factory, worked as his manager from 1674. The factory was given to him as a wedding present in 1678; its declared value was 4,000 guilders. Samuel never took an interest in other factories. It is probable that the magnificent bowls and other objects bearing the initials SVE are his work. The loose grouping of figures, as in the tea ceremony, *(ill. 36)* and the careful drawing of facial expressions and clothing are characteristic of his art. The blue-black or violet 'trek' or outline—probably his invention—accentuates the foliage of trees and bushes, while the shading of the glaze from light blue to grey-green and white indicates what careful attention he gave to the gradation of colours. After Samuel's death, his widow sold De Grieksche A to Adriaen Kocks, her brother-in-law, who was married to Judith van Eenhoorn and who further extended and increased the factory's high reputation. He managed it very successfully until his death in 1701. We know some of the names of the artists of that period, although we cannot attribute any specific works to them. They are Nicolaas de Weert, the manager, Jan Verburgh, a 'meesterplateelschilder' (master painter of pottery), who joined the factory in 1698 and Pieter van den Hurck who after working at De Dissel from 1694 moved to De Grieksche A in 1701. These and others were the real artists who succeeded in harmonizing Chinese and European design. Examples of this skill are a plate with a picture in the K'ang-hsi style and a Renaissance border and, conversely, a plate with the coat of arms of Jan van der Does, who married Elisabeth van der Dussen in 1677, which has a Chinese border. The latter was probably made for their twelfth wedding anniversary. Both plates bear Adriaen Kocks' mark *(ills. 37, 38)*.
Two water bottles decorated with mythological scenes and signed with the monogram AK represent a particularly high level of the artistic achievement. One of them represents Apollo pursuing Daphne, who transforms herself into a tree; it is elegantly framed by vines and garlands (Plate IX).

Ill. 35. Wine jug with handles decorated with a mountain landscape with children playing ball. Mark: IW (Jacob Wemmerson Hoppesteyn). Het Jonge Moriaenshooft, before 1670. Privately owned.

A royal commission for the palace at Hampton Court and its dairy gave De Grieksche A a special place among Delft factories. A bill dated 1695 documents the order by King William III which must have been commissioned between 1689 and 1694, the year in which Queen Mary died. It refers to a tiled room and tableware for the dairy, and to ornamental objects for the palace such as tall tulip vases with the motto and the coat of arms of the royal family, all of them executed according to sketches made by Daniel Marot, the king's French architect in The Hague. The tableware was also manufactured in the grand manner according to his designs (*ill. 40*). It is surprising how sparingly gold was used.

Until 1722, De Grieksche A developed as follows: Adriaen Kocks (d. 1701) was its director together with his son, Pieter Adriaenson. (This dual directorship is shown by two blue bottles, one of which is signed AK and the other PAK.) Pieter took over the factory one month after his father's death, but he himself died in 1703. The management was then left entirely in the hands of his widow, Johanna van der Heul, until she sold the business to Jacobus van der Kool on July 30, 1722. The years 1701—22 were the years of peak production, for which Johanna's husband and her father-in-law had laid the foundations, particularly because of the immediate success of the factory's imitations of Japanese Imari porcelain (see Chapter X). This became the factory's specialty. Johanna van der Heul managed this production expertly. The mark PAK continued to be used and the quality of the works of art and their wealth of decorative motifs remained at the same high level. Two objects, dated 1711 and 1715, indicate that the Imari style

Ill. 36. Small bottle-shaped vase depicting a Chinese tea ceremony in a landscape. Mark: SVE (Samuel van Eenhoorn). De Grieksche A, 1674—1686. The Hague, Gemeente Museum.

Ill. 37. Plate with Chinese decoration and European Renaissance border. Mark: AK (Adriaen Kocks). De Grieksche A, 1686–1701. Privately owned.

Ill. 38. Plate with the family coat of arms of Jan van der Does and Elisabeth van der Dussen, Chinese border. Mark: AK (Adriaen Kocks). De Grieksche A, 1686–1701. The Hague, Gemeente Museum.

Ill. 39. Large dish with a flower-pot as central motif and a six-part floral design. Mark: PAK (Peter Adriaenson Kocks). De Grieksche A, 1701—22. Arnhem, Gemeente Museum.

Ill. 40. Large blue and gold cream bowl. Mark: AK (Adriaen Kocks). De Grieksche A, 1695. Originally at Hampton Court Palace, now in London, Victoria and Albert Museum.

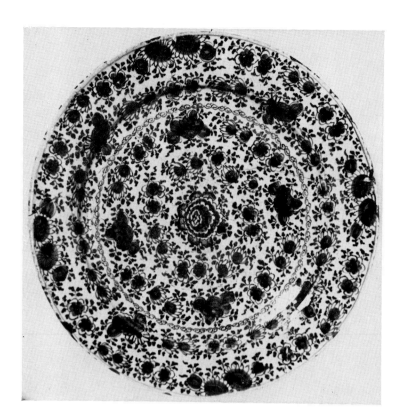

Ill. 41. Small plate with scattered floral pattern. Mark: JK (Johannes Knotter). De Porceleyne Fles, 1695–1701. Delft, Royal factory De Porceleyne Fles.

Ill. 42 Large bowl with four groups of Chinese figures in a landscape. Mark: SVE (Samuel van Eenhoorn). De Grieksche A, 1674–1686. Delft, Royal factory De Porceleyne Fles.

Plate X
Wig stand. Mark: LC (Lambert Cleffius). De Metalen Pot, 1670–91. Brussels, Musées royaux d'Art
et d'Histoire.

Plate XI
Harlequin. Mark: LVE (Lambert van Eenhorn).
De Metalen Pot, 1691–1721. Privately owned.

Ill. 43. Wig-stand representing a group of Chinese figures in a landscape. Mark: SVE (Samuel van Eenhoorn). London, Victoria and Albert Museum.

was used on blue dishes as well as on other objects. The artists working at De Grieksche A proved that their talents and taste lived up to the highest demands made on the Delft faience of that period. Johanna van der Heul was herself a qualified "plateelbakster" and excelled in particular in animal figures. Her works were signed J. v. d. H (Mark 62). A holy water basin (*ill. 44*) ornamented in the French style is an example of her work.

Ill. 44. Holy water basin. Mark: J. v. d. H. (Johanna van der Heul). De Grieksche A, 1701–22. (This piece was on the art market in 1965.)

De Porceleyne Fles (The Porcelain Bottle) *1653–1701*

These 'huysinge geapproprieert tot een plateelbackerye' (buildings which were transformed into a pottery factory in 1653) were not very successful until 1655 when Wouter van Eenhoorn together with Quirijn van Cleynhoven took over the factory and soon obtained better results. Van Cleynhoven managed the factory until his death in 1695. No works from that period are known.

Ill. 45. Bowl for spices or tea-bags, with Chinese decoration. Mark: LC (Lambert Cleffius). De Metalen Pot, 1670–91. Arnhem, Gemeente Museum.

Ill. 46. Oval four-legged plate with Chinese decoration. Mark: IVL (Jan van der Laan). De Metalen Pot (?), *c.* 1700. Privately owned.

His successor was Johannes Knotter, who was called a 'meester-porceleynbacker' and who was assisted by, among others, Dirk Baans, a 'meesterplateelschilder'. In the years which followed, De Porceleyne Fles could hold its own in any comparison with other factories. Johannes Knotter died in 1701 but despite his brief period as manager he contributed to the development of Delft, as is proven by a number of 'Kaapsche Schotels', various plates with blue or polychrome decoration and an octagonal pot with a scattered floral pattern in the manner of the fine plate (*ill. 41*) in which roses are arranged in circles. His works are signed with IK or JK, and a painted bottle next to it (Mark 34). We have no certain information dating from the time of Marcelis de Vlught (1701—50). Only later was De Porceleyne Fles to experience a new rise (see pages 132; 152).

Ill. 47. Water-bottle with stopper, scattered floral pattern. Mark: LVE (Lambert van Eenhoorn). De Metalen Pot, 1691—1721. The Hague, Gemeente Museum.

Ill. 48. Large jar with lid, decorated with scattered floral pattern. Mark: LVE and HKP (?) (Lambert van Eenhoorn and HKP (?)). De Metalen Pot, 1691–1721. Brussels, Musées royaux d'Art et d'Histoire.

De Metalen Pot (The Metal Pot) *1670–1721*

The ownership of this factory changed several times among associates whose names are known to us: for example the Cruyck family, Wouter van Eenhoorn and others, until 1670 when Willem Cleffius Sr bought the 'huysinge' from the representatives of the West India Company in Delft. Dirck Hieronymus van Kessel had already set up a pottery there, but Lambert Cleffius, Willem's son, who was registered in 1667 as a 'meester plateelbakker' in the books of the Guild of St Luke, took over De Metalen Pot and managed it until 1691. He claimed to have invented the technique for making red teapots as early as 1672 (Chapter VI). Lambert, Samuel van Eenhoorn and Quirijn van Cleynhoven were members of a delegation sent to England in 1684 after the fourth sea war with England (1682–84) in order to revive the export of Delft faience to that country. The inventory of his estate—he died in 1691—is an invaluable document. The objects bearing the initials LC, all of which are of careful and graceful workmanship, could either have been made by himself or manufactured in his factory. The painters who worked for him (we do not know any of their names) also showed an understanding of spatial relationships.

What is striking here is the sparing use of decoration, somewhat in the style of Samuel van Eenhoorn. This also holds true for colours and glaze. A wig stand (Plate X) and a bowl for spices or teabags, presumably small bags containing different kinds of tea (*ill. 45*) convey the refinement of Cleffius's style. We have already referred to the 'Kaapsche Schotels' which he made.

One should also mention his collaborator, Lambert van Eenhoorn, who became his successor in

Ill. 49. Two tall tulip vases. Mark: IVL (Jan van der Laan). De Metalen Pot (?), *c.* 1700. Amsterdam, Rijksmuseum.

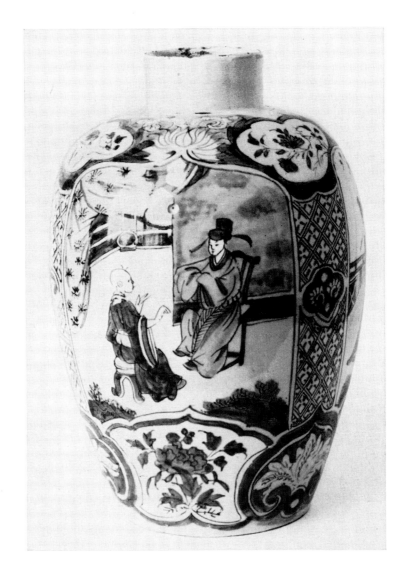

1691, when he acquired De Metalen Pot for 9,500 guilders from Lambert Cleffius's heirs. Lambert van Eenhoorn, one of Wouter's sons, must have been a cause of anxiety to his family:
after roaming for many years through Europe and the Dutch East Indies, after poor management
and a settlement in his favour, records dating from 1689 refer to him as 'jegenswoordigh
porceleynbacker' (at present a maker of porcelain). Yet it is he who gave the name of the
factory its reputation and increased it even further when, after the turn of the century, polychrome
faience became very popular. He died in 1721. It was not until 1724 that his widow sold the
enterprise to Cornelis Coppens (d. 1761) who until that time was an unknown figure in Delft
industry.

LVE, Lambert van Eenhoorn's factory mark (Mark 108), provoked a violent quarrel with a
competitor which lasted from 1691 until 1713, possibly even until 1735. Victor Victorson and his

Ill. 51. Two roosters. Mark: LVE (Lambert van Eenhoorn). De Metalen Pot, 1691–1721. Privately owned.

Ill. 52. Plate with Chinese decoration. Border subdivided like an aureole. Mark: LVF (Louwijs Victorson Fecit) and DS (Dobbelde Schenckan). De Dobbelde Schenckan, 1688–1713. Brussels, Musées royaux d'Art et d'Histoire.

Ill. 53. Small plate with Chinese decoration radially arranged, plants and standing figures. Mark: LVF (Louwijs Victorson Fecit) and AK (unknown painter). De Dobbelde Schenckan, 1688–1713. (On the art market in 1965.)

Ill. 54. Plate representing Jacob's dream, border decoration of angels on clouds. Mark: the small gothic letter r. De Roos (Arent Cosijn), 1675–80. London, Victoria and Albert Museum.

Ill. 55. Octagonal bottle-shaped vase representing Christ and several apostles; on the neck of the bottle, angels on clouds. No mark, probably from De Roos factory, *c.* 1700. Rotterdam, Boymans van Beuningen Museum.

son Louwijs, the owners of De Dobbelde Schenckan (The Double Jug) had been using a similar monogram, namely the initials LVF (Marks 128, 129). (The father died in 1713, while the son continued as the head of the factory until 1735 when it passed into other hands.) This dispute was probably the reason why the initials of the 'plateelschilder en -bakker' were added to the factory mark, by means of which the origin of the works of art can still be determined today. Both factories produced objects of exemplary beauty in blue as well as in polychrome faience.

We will limit ourselves to a consideration of the blue faience produced by De Metalen Pot. Cornelis van der Klout worked there, while Johannes van der Wal was the manager and was replaced only in 1695 by Jan Verburgh. All were well-known painters. The discovery of the initials

Ill. 56. Large gourd-shaped vase with Chinese decoration. Six panels with figures and plants. Mark: GK (Gerrit Kam). De Paeuw, 1701–05 or De 3 Vergulde Aston-nekens, 1680–1705. The Hague, Gemeente Museum.

HIP in the records was of great importance for polychrome faience (see page 83). The initials HPK or HIPK, which have not yet been explained, belong to the painter of two particularly impressive vases with a scattered floral pattern and of a water bottle with a stopper (*ills. 47, 48*). It is a possibility that Jan van der Laan whose monogram is IVL (Marks 77, 79) was one of the painters at De Metalen Pot. He had a marked preference for large oval dishes, some of them with a matching water pitcher, which he decorated with Chinese pictures representing ceremonial receptions, terraces and the like (*ill. 46*). Two tall tulip vases in the shape of obelisks are also among his works (*ill. 49*). De Metalen Pot was also the first to make figures representing human beings and animals. The pilloried harlequin shows the Dutch sense of realism (Plate XI). The two roosters (*ill. 51*) were meant to be salt and pepper shakers.

Ill. 57. Large jar with lid and Chinese decoration. Flower bouquets in four medallions. Mark: De Paeuw (attributed to Lambert Cleffius). De Paeuw, 1662–80. Arnhem, Gemeente Museum.

De Dobbelde Schenckan (The Double Jug) *1661–1713*

This factory was of special, if short-lived, significance in the history of Delft faience. It was founded in 1661, but only became well-known when its owner Dirck Jansz van Schie, who decided to go to Kassel to work, sold it in 1688 to Victor Victorson and his son Louwijs. Their ownership was the only important period in the history of this factory. Victor died in 1713 and his son remained as head of the factory until 1735. Shortly after that it sank into oblivion and was liquidated in 1777.

In spite of the confusing resemblance of factory marks, clear decorative and figurative distinctions can be established by a comparison of objects manufactured in De Metalen Pot and in De Dobbelde Schenckan, as far as they can be attributed with certainty to the one or the other. The latter followed the original K'ang-hsi decoration more faithfully, and showed a definite preference for white design on a blue background which alternated with small blue flourishes on a white background. A tulip vase dating from the year 1704 is particularly characteristic of this pottery (Plate XII). The objects bearing the initials IP (Jan Pieterson, journeyman and pottery painter) demonstrate his talent for shaping and painting, and very closely rivalling Chinese porcelain (*ill. 50*). This factory also produced large and small plates with Chinese decorations and a striking delicacy in figure design. These plates are of a high artistic quality. We know that artists other than Jan Pieterson worked in this pottery and, although we know only their initials, their work deserves mention (*ills. 52, 53*). In addition we know that the polychrome faience made in this factory had many new features (see page 84) so that De Dobbelde Schenckan should rightly be given a special place among Delft factories during the period in which the Victorsons ran it.

De Roos (The Rose) *1662–1712*

This factory deserves to be mentioned at this point even though its products have a character all their own. It only began to operate in 1667 when Ir Soubreé was the manager. Hendrick Janzon Peridon studied here as 'schildersgast' (apprentice painter) from 1698 to 1702; some of the polychrome works of art made by him for De Metalen Pot are discussed below. The owners of De Roos were Arent Cosijn (from before 1675 to 1680), Nicolaeson Janson van Straten, a member of a family of well-known potters (1680–1694) and Dammas Hofdijk (1694–1712). A definite preference for religious subjects was shown in this factory both in its coarser earthenware and its genuine faience; some particularly splendid faience plates have been preserved. They depict episodes from the Old and the New Testaments. The development of De Roos can be deduced from them, as well as

Ill. 58. Large plate depicting Christ in front of Pilate. Mark: De Roos. Early 18th century. Private collection.

from the factory marks (see page 160) which at first consisted of the small gothic letter R (Arent Cosijn and Van Straten) and later of 'Roos' written in cursive letters (1727–1755). On the underside of small tea caddies one also finds as a mark, under the glaze, the capital letter R framed by a diamond made of four small dots (Mark 120). This symbol points to another painter (H. S. ?) whose name we also do not know. The plate representing Jacob's dream (*ill. 54*) is one of the most beautiful of the religiously inspired works. Seven plates of this kind are known to exist, all of them painted in the manner of various engravings, some of which were the work of Lucas van Leyden (1494–1536). The border is decorated with angels on clouds, a motif which can be traced back to a banderole with climbing flowers dating from the year 1509. An octagonal bottle-shaped vase representing the suffering Christ and several apostles and angels is a variation on the same theme (*ill. 55*). Under later owners this factory achieved a high reputation for the production of polychrome faience (see Chapter VII).

De Paeuw (The Peacock) *1651–1705*

We possess evidence of the work of this factory (which was bought in 1651 by Hieronymus von Kessel for 12,500 guilders) in the form of a blue plate with the portrait of St Eligius, the patron saint of goldsmiths, with a metal rim and the inscription 'Claes Janse Messchaert 1653'. Messchaert was originally a pewterer in Rotterdam who came to Delft because he was Van Kessel's son-in-law; however, his wife died as early as 1652. He was still mentioned as a 'porceleynbacker' in 1656, but in 1659 he is referred to as a 'gewezen plattielbacker in De Paeuw' (former master potter in the Peacock). He had taken over the brewery belonging to his second wife. Steven Dirckson van Kessel became the De Paeuw manager in 1659 (?) but had to make way for the new owners in 1662; one half of the factory belonged to Gijsbrecht Lambrechtson Cruyck, the other half was shared by Willem Cleffius and Wouter van Eenhoorn. The latter soon handed his share over to Lambert Cleffius. No objects made in the years 1662–1680 can at present be definitely attributed to this pottery. The potters and painters of this period are unknown and Lambert and Willem Cleffius were simultaneously the owners of De Paeuw and De Metalen Pot so that their factory mark by itself does not indicate in which pottery a piece was made.

In 1701 De Paeuw became the property of the Kam family. From 1668 Gerrit Kam was half-owner of De 3 Vergulde Astonnekens (The Three Golden Ash-Barrels) and became its sole owner after Wouter van Eenhoorn's death when he transferred the factory to his eldest son, Pieter. (His youngest son, David, is discussed in Chapter VIII.) In 1701 Gerrit became the owner of De Paeuw and from this date we can identify his work. We know, however, that he was highly considered by his fellow craftsmen before this time as he was a member of the committee of Delft potters which, on July 27, 1684, sent Samuel van Eenhoorn, Quirijn van Cleynhoven and Lambert Cleffius to the King of England to revive trade in Delft faience.

It must be assumed that the works by Gerrit and Pieter Kam (who both died in 1705) which we know were manufactured in De 3 Vergulde Astonnekens rather than De Paeuw. The father's work is distinguished by his precise imitation of the K'ang-hsi style and by the new shapes he gave to his vases. *Illustration 56* shows a gourd-shaped vase, the surface of which has been artfully subdivided, and stylized plants and figures which are carefully drawn and coloured dark blue. Pieter Kam's work, on the contrary, is purely decorative. His style is characterized by clearly arranged geometrical groupings and a sense of rich ornamentation and skillful gradations of colour (Plate XIII).

The large jar with a lid exhibited in the Gemeente Museum in Arnhem — which only bears the mark of De Paeuw (Mark 102) — must be attributed to Lambert Cleffius for stylistic reasons. The design bears no resemblance to the motifs usually employed by Gerrit or Pieter Kam. For this very reason the pot is valuable for us, because it proves to us that the artistry of the 'plateelschilders' also contributes to the identification of works of art (*ill. 57*).

This discussion of seven of the best-known faience factories proves the extent to which the Delft factories had perfected their workmanship in the period between 1670 and 1730. The remaining thirty factories worked by no means less well. The international fame achieved by the Delft factories with their blue faience was well deserved. If we also remember the variety of polychrome faience fired at high or low temperatures (see Chapters VIII and X) and that numerous unsigned objects of the highest quality have been preserved, the technical, stylistic or historical origin of which we cannot determine, then we can get some indication of how important the Delft faience industry was.

VI. Red Delft Teapots: 1672–1731

After 1670 Delft potters experimented with what the inventories term 'rode Delftse trekpotjes' (red Delft teapots). These have a special place in the history of Delft pottery mainly because of the technique which was evolved in manufacturing them and the material which was used.

Drinking tea had become a common custom in the Netherlands. The tea was imported from China, as were red Chinese teapots, and experience showed that the tea's aroma and heat were best preserved in these pots. Delft potters attempted, therefore, to imitate these pots but copying them turned out to be a difficult process. It was known that materially they consisted of two basic substances in powder form which melted at different temperatures: red 'bole', which is hard to fuse, and lean clay which is easy to fuse and which takes on a dull sheen when polished after being fired. Ideally the teapots should not be porous, and yet they were not glazed.

How this type of pot was produced was the secret of the Chinese potters: something similar was, however, achieved in Delft. This was a red substance with a matte glaze, a type of stoneware known as 'gres' or 'boccaro' which resembled porcelain. The craftsmen specializing in it were known as 'theepotbackers' (makers of teapots). They publicized their invention extensively and competed keenly with each other. The first advertisement for this product, by Lambert Cleffius, is found in the *Haarlemse Courant*, August 18, 1678. He asserts that he has 'maecken van roode Theepotten ... tot sodanighe perfectie heeft gebracht, dat dezelve in couleur, netheyt, sterckte em gebruyck de Indische niet behoeven te wijcken ...' (achieved such perfection in the manufacturing of red teapots that they are in no way inferior in colour, purity and durability to the Indian teapots). We do not know any of the red teapots made by Lambert Cleffius (d. 1691) nor any of those made by his successor, Lambert van Eenhoorn (d. 1721). The latter, however, is known to have hired a trained wood-carver, Guillaume Neuillet of Le Havre, who, according to his contract dated April 25, 1691, was to make red teapots 'soo konstigh ende goet als hij sal kennen, sonder dat hij bij off voor iemand anders sal moghen wercken' (as artistically and well as he possibly could, without working with or for another employer). This contract was renewed for another ten years in 1693, but the designs remained the property of De Metalen Pot, as did the red teapots and 'andere rariteyten' (other curiosities). This latter phrase probably refers to very small red figurines which were listed in the inventory as '2 beeldetjes, 5 kleine dito' (two statuettes and five similar red ones).

In spite of the large stock which must have been manufactured by Neuillet, we know of only two examples with Lambert van Eenhoorn's mark, one of them being a teapot (*ill. 59*) decorated with

Plate XII
Tulip vase. Mark: DS 1704 (Louwijs Victorson).
De Dobbelde Schenckan, 1688–1713. Marssum,
Popta State Castle, Friesland.

Plate XIII
Large jar with lid and Chinese decoration. Eight
panels with flower bouquets. Mark: PK (Pieter
Kam). De 3 Vergulde Astonnekens, 1701–05. Brussels, Musées royaux d'Art et d'Histoire.

Ill. 59. Red stoneware teapot. Mark: A leaping unicorn with a star above it, impressed on an oval medallion surrounded by the inscription 'Lamb. van Eenhorn'. De Metalen Pot, 1691–1724. Groningen, Groninger Museum van Stad en Lande.

the relief of a plum tree branch. The mark is oval and represents a leaping unicorn with a star above it, surrounded by the inscription 'Lamb. van Eenhoorn'.

Ary de Milde acquired, justifiably, greater fame for his Delft teapots and we can follow his career thanks to well-presevered records. On June 11, 1658, he was registered as a member of the Guild of St Luke and until 1665 he was the manager of De Grieksche A under Wouter van Eenhoorn. To date none of his work from this period is known. In 1671 we know that he and Martinus Gouda each bought half of De Romeyn (see also Chapter VIII) but he remained there only one year, leaving

Ill. 60. Red 'porcelain' teapot, mounted in silver. Mark: A fox running toward the left impressed on an oval medallion surrounded by the inscription 'Arey de Milde'. De Gecroonde Theepot, 1680–1708. Privately owned.

to specialize in the firing of red teapots. A document, dated 1677, testifies to his devotion to his craft. His landlord had asked him whether he wished to remain in the house to which he replied: 'Ja, als gij mij houden wilt, het is mijn gelegenheyt niet te verhuysen om de vele van mij gemaeckte oventjes, ick sal blijven' (Yes, if you are willing to have me. I do not intend to move because of the many kilns built by me. I shall stay on.) He attempted to achieve the degree of hardness and water-tightness of Chinese 'rood porceleyn-theepotjes' (red porcelain teapots); that is, to produce something different from the 'boccaro' or 'gres' as originally made by Cleffius, Lambert van Eenhoorn and, perhaps, by himself as well. All three men competed violently to be the first to manufacture these teapots. This competition is documented by a petition submitted to the Staten

Ill. 61. Red stoneware teapot, mounted with silver. Mark: A running doe impressed on an oval medallion surrounded by the inscription 'Jacobus de Caluwe 1701–1730'. Amsterdam, Rijksmuseum.

Ill. 62. Left: Very small teapot of red stoneware. No mark, probably the work of D. W. F. de Rotte or Peter de Lorreyn. Before 1731. Groningen, Groninger Museum van Stad en Lande.

Right: Red stoneware teapot. Mark: A leaping fox impressed on an oval medallion surrounded by the inscription 'D. W. F. Rotte'. Beginning of the 18th century. Groningen, Groninger Museum van Stad en Lande.

Ill. 63. Red 'porcelain' teapot with polychrome ornamentation and red pomegranates. Mark: A fox running toward the left impressed on an oval medallion surrounded by the inscription 'Arey de Milde'. Arnhem, Gemeente Museum.

van Hollan in 1679 by De Milde and Samuel van Eenhoorn in which they requested a fifteen-year patent or, if this were impossible, the protection of their products by a factory mark. The latter request was granted in 1680.

The mark deposited by Ary de Milde—an oval medallion—was used by him only once, on March 12, 1680, just after the decree of the Staten. The mark on the other works of his which have been preserved is a fox running toward the left (Mark 148, *ill. 60*). He also signed, with a crowned teapot, the name of his factory, De Gecroonde Theepot (The Crowned Teapot), which earlier had been known as The Juniper Tree. The Gemeente Museum in Arnhem owns an octagonal bowl on the front of which a crowned teapot is embossed and over it what remains of the name: '. . . DE MILDE'. The flat part of the bowl has been filled in with acanthus vines (*ill. 64*). After 1687 the records refer to De Milde on several occasions as 'meester theepotbacker'.

De Milde's works can also be related to the invention of red porcelain in Dresden in 1708. It can now probably be considered certain that Böttger and von Tschirnhause invented European porcelain together. The latter visited De Milde in Delft in 1701 and it has been said that De Milde gave him information about the composition of the Delft material. It has even been suggested that De Milde gave Tschirnhause the secrets of his process. Whatever the facts of this, the experiments conducted in Dresden were unsuccessful until February 1708 when a German potter named Rüllener, who had been instructed by De Milde, went to Dresden. Shortly afterwards red porcelain was successfully manufactured. The fact that a few examples of Delft red teapots, both from Lambert van Eenhoorn and from Ary de Milde, were available certainly had a bearing on this success.

Another theory, advanced by Miss M. A. de Visser, an authority on the subject, credits De Milde with being the inventor of 'rood porceleyne'. She asserted that some of the 'trekpotjes' which

Ill. 64. Octagonal bowl, so-called 'pattipan'. Mark: A teapot with a crown embossed on the front and surrounded by the inscription '...DE MILDE'. De Gecroonde Theepot, 1680–1708. Arnhem, Gemeente Museum.

today are in museums in Dresden, Gotha, Arnhem and Groningen are, in fact, imitations made by Böttger from original models. He is supposed to have copied them even to the extent of reproducing the original factory marks. Polychrome teapots, such as the one shown in *illustration 63*, on which pomegranates form the core of the flowers are considered by Miss de Visser as examples of the kind of object which Böttger imitated. If Miss de Visser's theory is true then De Milde was the first to develop the correct fusion process.

Red teapots were manufactured in Delft by different factories until about 1730. De Metalen Pot ceased this production about 1724 in which year Guillaume Neuillet died (Lambert van Eenhoorn had died in 1721). Ary de Milde died in 1708, but his daughter, who had married Willem Lardijn, continued to manage De Gecroonde Theepot until January 3, 1724.

Jacobus de Caluwe (d. 1730) is another teapot maker whose name appears in the records in 1702, 1710 and 1713. He worked in the dilapidated building of the former De Dissel factory which had been abandoned in 1701 and reverted to its original use as a brewery. His teapots are signed with a running doe impressed on an oval medallion surrounded by the inscription 'Jacobus de Caluwe'. Their quality is not as outstanding as that of the pieces made by De Milde. De Caluwe also decorated his teapots with plum tree branches, but subdivided their surfaces into diamond-shaped panels which he outlined with dots made by a small-toothed wheel. *Illustration 61* shows an example of his work. This piece has a particularly beautiful silver chain and a figure on the lid. Miss de Visser's recent research has revealed the names of two more Delft 'theepotbakkers'—W. F. de Rotte and Peter de Lorreyn. Although De Rotte's name appears in records he is not specifically referred to as 'theepotbakker'. We know three pieces made by him, but only one which can be attributed certainly to Peter de Lorreyn (in the collection of Prince von Salm-Salm in Anholt). De Lorreyn was called a 'plateeldraaier' (wheel-driver and potter) in 1721 and in 1727 a 'potjes-bakker' (skilled potter); he died in 1731. (De Rotte's dates are not known.) De Lorreyn and De Rotte used the same motifs and both had as their mark a vertical medallion impressed with a fox leaping toward the left and their name above it. In 1954 the Groninger Museum acquired De Rotte's red teapot and the small unsigned red teapot (*ill. 62*).

The very small teapots were used to taste various kinds of tea at the time when it became fashionable to pour tea at ladies' gatherings. Housewives bought their tea at apothecaries (tea was still considered a medicine by many) and would bring with them a small pot to taste the different varieties. These small teapots were not only made of 'rood porceleyn'; they were also manufactured with polychrome or yellow floral designs on black or olive-green backgrounds (see Chapter VIII and *ill. 86*).

VII. Polychrome Delft Faience Fired at High Temperatures: 1670—1730

Het Jonge Moriaenshooft

We know for certain that the mark IW, belonging to Jacob Wemmerson Hoppesteyn, was used after his death in 1671 during the period in which his widow, who died in 1686, managed the factory. Her son, Rochus, was only nineteen years old when he acquired the title 'meester plateel-schilder' in 1680 and he must have shown signs of an unusual talent while he was being trained (possibly in his father's factory). As has been mentioned above it is not unlikely that the blue and white, as well as the polychrome, vine decoration was Rochus's innovation.

As well as this early contribution to ornamentation we find in Rochus's work a masterly representation of Chinese motifs, executed in polychrome and gilding. Dr H. E. van Gelder's research into

Ill. 65. A polygonal dish, originally part of a reistafel service. Polychrome with gold, Chinese decoration. Mark: RIHS (Rochus Hoppesteyn). Het Jonge Moriaenshooft, 1680—92. Amsterdam, Rijksmuseum.

Ill. 66. Jug with handle. Chinese decoration, polychrome with gilding. Mark: RIHS (Rochus Hoppesteyn) and Moriaenshooft. Het Jonge Moriaenshooft, 1680–92. Brussels, Musées royaux d'Art et d'Histoire.

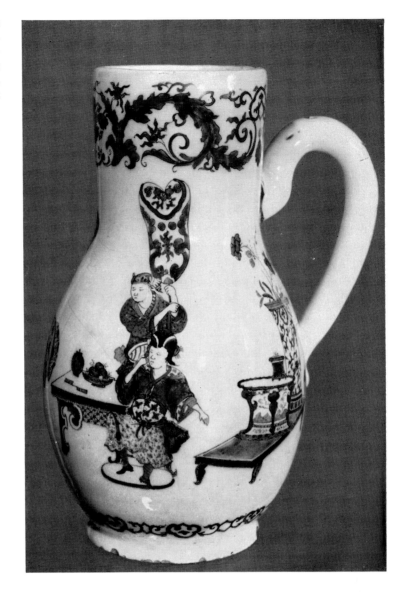

records has revealed an explanation of Rochus's skill in this field. During this period commissions were given to painters who worked at home and among these was Jeremias Theunison Godtling who was mentioned in records in 1664 and 1667. In 1668 he worked in The Hague in a factory (which received financial assistance from the city council) together with a painter from Delft, Willem van der Lith, who was the manager, and a silversmith, Nicolaes Cornelison Keyser, who was a partner. This enterprise was kept strictly confidential particularly with respect to the art of 'porceleynbackerye met gout, root ende andere couleuren by haer uytgevonden' (firing porcelain with gold, red and other colours which were invented there). Records dating from 1692 and 1694 indicate that Rochus Hoppesteyn had made a contract with Van der Lith and Godtling 'omtrent het maecken ende backen van porceleynen met gout beschildert' (in order to manufacture and fire

porcelain painted with gold). This was stated by the administrator of Rochus's estate in accounting for its bankruptcy in July 1694.

Between 1680 and his death in 1692 Rochus was manager and owner of Het Jonge Moriaenshooft and works marked with a Moor's head and the initials RIHS (Marks 92, 93) can be attributed to him. It cannot, however, be proved that they did not originate in The Hague and were painted and fired there. An idea of the outstanding quality of Rochus's work is given by the small dish (*ill. 65*) which belonged to a 'reistafel' (rice table) service and a jug (*ill. 66*). They are among the very rare pieces of polychrome Delft faience using low-temperature colours made before the muffle-kiln technique had been evolved which can be called works of art.

Plate XIV
Polychrome oval plaque with Chinese decoration
on black background. No mark, c. 1700. Privately
owned.

As we have noted, Lieven van Dalen took over Het Jonge Moriaenshooft after the death of Rochus Hoppesteyn and it seems that several 'plateelschilders' remained at the factory and continued to paint in the style of Hoppesteyn although they could not achieve the same quality. The influence of Hoppesteyn may be demonstrated by several pieces, including some polychrome bottle-shaped vases, each of which is decorated with three medallions framed by arabesques (*ills. 67, 68*). Each of the vases depicts contemporary European scenes: a dancing couple accompanied by a violinist and a cellist; a guitar player and two ladies playing the lute at a table; a waitress serving wine and cakes to three ladies sitting at a table. The border designs around the medallions are characteristic of Hoppesteyn's style but all of the figures shown are dressed in post-1700 fashion; this is proved by, among other things, the ladies hair style which is topped by a lace 'fontange'. A small polychrome

Ill. 68. The other vase belonging to the set. (See *Ill. 67.*). Privately owned.

73

Ill. 69. Small polychrome bowl with European decoration, polychrome with gilding. Mark: IW (Jacob Wemmerson). Attributed to Het Jonge Moriaenshooft, *c.* 1710. The Hague, Nijstad Antiquairs NV.

Ill. 70. Oval container used as a wine cooler, decorated with flower garlands and angel figures. Mark: PAK (Pieter Adraenson Kocks). De Grieksche A, 1701–22. Privately owned.

Ill. 71. Large dish with flower design and a representation of Flora. Mark: PAK (Pieter Adraenson Kocks). De Grieksche A, 1701—22. Arnhem, Gemeente Museum.

Ill. 72. Oval bowl with lid. Decorated with Chinese plant motif. Mark: De Dissel; it was however manufactured in De Grieksche A, *c.* 1725. Privately owned.

Ill. 73.　Jug with four medallions
on a green background. Mark: De
Dissel; it was however manufactured in De Grieksche A, *c.*
1725. The Hague, Gemeente Museum.

bowl, 12 cm. in diameter (*ill. 69*) is another example of the Hoppesteyn influence. The bowl represents a group of two ladies and two gentlemen drinking from 'trembleuses'—chocolate cups with
deep saucers, of which only a very few examples made of black faience have been preserved. (*ill.
89* shows a 'trembleuse'). The chocolate pot stands on a tall decorative table. The bowl bears the
mark IW (Jacob Wemmerson) but it must be dated to the early eighteenth century. The work of
Lieven van Dalen differs too much from that of the Hoppesteyns to be discussed here and will be
considered in Chapter VIII.

Ill. 74. Large bowl with Chinese decoration. Mark: The monogram PVD and the date (?) 1721. Factory unknown, 1721. The Hague, Gemeente Museum.

Ill. 75. Set of three very large lidded Kashmir vases with vine decoration. Mark: Roos. De Roos, *c.* 1725. Rotterdam, Boymans van Beuningen Museum.

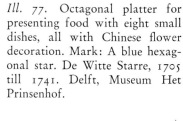

Ill. 76. Oval bowl with Chinese flower decoration. Mark: LVE and HIP (Lambert van Eenhoorn and Hendrick Janson Peridon). De Metalen Pot, 1691–1721. Arnhem, Gemeente Museum.

Ill. 77. Octagonal platter for presenting food with eight small dishes, all with Chinese flower decoration. Mark: A blue hexagonal star. De Witte Starre, 1705 till 1741. Delft, Museum Het Prinsenhof.

Ill. 78. Two large ornamental pots with Chinese flower decoration and large leaf pattern. Mark: LVE (Lambert van Eenhoorn). De Metalen Pot, 1691–1721. Amsterdam, Rijksmuseum.

Ill. 79. Group of seven small vases, with Chinese decoration, consisting of a jar with lid, two tumblers, two bottles and two gourd-shaped vases. Mark: LVF and IP (Louwijs Victorson and Jan Pieterson). De Dobbelde Schenckan, 1688–1713. Privately owned.

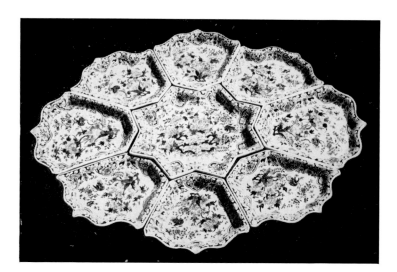

De Grieksche A

The so-called 'Hoppesteyn technique' may have been the first, but was by no means the only one, to be developed around the year 1700. After all, polychrome Delft faience evolved from the majolica of earlier years and as in the case of tiles a gradual refinement of technique can be observed. The use of containers during the firing process helped considerably to achieve better results with colours since they no longer ran, while the lead glaze mixture—the 'kwaart'—gave a particular sheen to the object. The problems inherent in the use of red and gold remained unsolved, however, until the muffle technique had been perfected (see Chapter X).

Moreover, at the turn of the century great stylistic changes and new influences made themselves felt of which manifold use was made in the manufacturing of polychrome Delft faience. In addition to the K'ang-hsi porcelain, the craftsmen came to know French pottery, mainly the type made in Rouen. As a result a much greater variety in dishes and decorative objects developed.

After 1700, De Grieksche A became one of the best-known factories. Its historical development under the ownership of Adriaen Kocks, his son Pieter and his widow, Johanna van der Heul, who sold it in 1722, has already been mentioned. PAK, the monogram of Pieter Adriaenson Kocks continued to be used after his death. We know several polychrome plates dating from that period, some of which show great similarity to the ones with blue decoration, as for instance the plate with

flower bouquets turned towards the centre. Only here the rosette is replaced by a representation of Flora sitting among shrubs and holding flower bouquets in her raised hands (*ill. 71*). This is probably a new motif, which was copied frequently later on.

Undoubtedly one of the most important finds from this period is a very rare wine cooler on four short legs with two lions' heads as handles. The sidewalls and the bottom on the inside are decorated in the Italian manner with a series of angel figures floating and playing among flower garlands. The cooler is signed in bold strokes of the brush with the monogram PAK (*ill. 70*). Besides the designs of its own very able painters, De Grieksche A used, well into the eighteenth century, the mod-

Ill. 80. Octagonal jar with lid and Chinese vine decoration. Mark: Roos. De Roos, *c.* 1725. Rotterdam, Boymans van Beuningen Museum.

Plate XV
Large blue tile from the dairy at Hampton Court
Palace (1689–94). Mark: AK (Adriaen Kocks).
De Grieksche A, 1686–1701. Amsterdam, Rijks-
museum.

Plate XVI
Oval plaque with architectural decoration. No
mark. Attributed to Adriaen Kocks. De Grieksche
A, c. 1712. The Hague, Gemeente Museum.

Ill. 81. One of two square tea caddies depicting Chinese landscapes and figures. No mark, *c.* 1725. Privately owned.

els which Adriaen Kocks took over from De Dissel factory together with all its remaining possessions: the factory mark, a shaft or a line resembling it, with the letter D (Marks 27, 28, 29) was retained. Besides countless decorative plates of different sizes, we have a rare example of such an object bearing the De Dissel mark in a splendid bowl with a lid (*ill. 72*). Its decoration is technically 'mille fleurs'. On the plates, the medallion features a flower basket surrounded by panels, each of which has in its right-hand corner a similar plant which spreads its branches and blossoms over the white surface. The bowl is also subdivided into panels, but in this case the plants are turned alternately to the right or the left to follow its oval shape, thus making for a particularly well-balanced composition.

A polychrome jug bears a similar mark; its particular quality is due to its careful design. It could

Ill. 82. One of two plaques with polychrome flower bouquets framed in black. No mark, 1700—25. Privately owned.

be considered as one of the so-called 'heart patterns', which later became very popular for decorative plates, although the execution of the design was by then usually much less meticulous. In this particular case however, the four medallions (the outlines of medallions really were drawn in the shape of a heart during a later period) make for the special charm of this pattern with their polychrome bouquets, plants and trees against white shading into blue, the moss-green curved background and the fashionable dark leaf ornamentation (*ill. 73*). If one compares this design with the heart-pattern plates, one can see a certain resemblance but also a distinct difference in the composition as well as in the quality. Some of these plates are signed with the initials IVL which are attributed to Jan van der Laan. Research into the archives has shown that in 1675 a certain Jan Janson van der Laan worked as 'plateelbakker' in De 3 Klokken (The Three Clocks) and in 1693 Jan van der Laan is mentioned as a 'meester porcelleynbakker' in the 't Hart (The Heart) factory. Both enterprises were run by the Mesch (Mes) family: 't Hart from 1661 to 1745 and De 3 Klokken from 1670 to 1725. Since further details are lacking we must content ourselves for the time being with this and the possible attribution of the initials IVL. There are also several large plates decorated with heart pattern and signed with the initials AK or AVK; however neither in period nor in style can they be attributed to Adriaen Kocks even if his mark were to have continued to be used for some time. Nor is there any point in ascribing them to a certain Anthony Kruisweg of whom no other object is known. The problems we have mentioned only prove that the factories frequently used the same models and that it still is not possible to attribute objects to any one factory with absolute certainty.

The same questions arise with respect to the 'mille fleurs' plates, as for instance in the case of a splendid polychrome bowl (*ill. 74*) on which the surface is divided into eight parts and decorated with flowering plants; flowering plants are depicted in the eight border panels. The central medallion represents a wild dog or a mythical beast on a rock, above which a bird is circling. This centre motif is surrounded by a wreath of stylized flowers — light against a dark background — where the same animal in two different positions is repeated eight times inside a circle. The decoration of this bowl is executed to perfection; the harmony of its colours enhances this impression. In this case, the signature is JVD and the year 1721. We know neither the full name of the artist who decorated it nor where it was made. However, the date 1721 on the bowl permits us to date the similar objects mentioned above to the same period.

The foregoing indicates how prominent a position De Grieksche A occupied after the year 1700. It should also be mentioned that with the development of the muffle technique, *i.e.,* the firing of objects at low temperatures, the factory's production and reputation increased even further.

De Metalen Pot

In contrast to De Grieksche A, this factory, as far as we know, never fired objects in the muffle kiln. On the contrary, Lambert van Eenhoorn distinguished himself by making polychrome Delft faience with colours fired at a high temperature. The numerous works of art made by him which have been preserved give an almost complete record of production by this method. Mention should first be made of the Kashmir vases and of a group of large vases, consisting of three pots with lids and two vases decorated with a Chinese flower pattern on a rippled surface. They were the crowning ornament of Dutch baroque cupboards. Their colouration was enhanced by violet and yellow. This vigorous style can be seen in two large ornamental pots for terraces from Lambert van Eenhoorn's factory (*ill. 78*). They combine various elements of style: the Kashmir ripples are used next to the graceful Chinese flower decoration; the baroque relief of dark green fan-shaped leaves is set off against the involuted handles which promptly bring to mind French designs of the year 1700 and, in this instance particularly, the pottery made in Rouen. (There was also an influence in the other direction: in historical studies of French pottery the influence of Delft faience is given similar recognition.)

Research into archives has provided the name of one 'plateelschilder' who worked in Lambert van Eenhoorn's factory, De Metalen Pot. His initials — HIP — stand for Hendrick Janson Peridon, born in 1640. Around the year 1665 he worked for about four years as 'schildersgast' in the De Roos factory and in 1672 we find him in 't Fortuyn; his name is also mentioned in records dating from the years 1678, 1709 and 1710, although we do not know for whom he worked at these dates. He joined Lambert van Eenhoorn in 1702 and it is likely that he remained at De Metalen Pot until his death in 1722. We know mainly polychrome objects made by him. A deep oval bowl, also executed in the Kashmir technique and decorated with a polychrome scattered flower pattern (*ill. 76*), may be cited as an example of his work. The five works by Hendrick Peridon known to us at present, among which is a group of three Kashmir vases, show a richly varied subdivision of space which resembles the K'ang-hsi style.

De Dobbelde Schenckan

Thanks to the initials IP which stand for Jan Pieterson, 'meesterknecht en plateelschilder' (master-apprentice pottery painter) who worked for Louwijs Victorson in De Dobbelde Schenckan, we are in a position to ascribe polychrome faience with certainty to this factory. To the masterpieces produced in this factory belong the odd group of seven small Kashmir vases, in which the jar with a lid is marked with the initials of the factory and of the artist (*ill. 79*). The distribution of the motif, the flowering branches which sometimes are painted in different breadths according to the size of the panel, is particularly clever. Although it would be difficult to produce conclusive evidence, one is tempted, in a comparison of certain works of art originating from either De Dobbelde Schenckan or De Metalen Pot, to attribute to De Dobbelde Schenckan those objects whose pattern, design, colour and glaze are of better quality, particulary if it is a matter of the stylistic evaluation of the objects signed with the controversial monogram LVE or LVF.

De Roos

During the peak period of blue Delft faience this factory, which was then managed by Arent Cosijn and Dammas Hofdijk, had held a unique place because of its specialization in religious subjects. It later developed, mainly while it was under the management of the Van Dijk family, a particular style of polychrome faience. Abraham van Dijk bought the factory in 1712. He died in 1727 and in 1732 his widow married Jacob de Milde and managed the enterprise with him until his death in 1739. Cornelis van Dijk then took over the family property until 1755. They all contributed to the great esteem in which De Roos was held; not the least of the reasons for this being the unique tile pictures in polychrome and black Delft faience produced in this factory (see Chapter IX). It is therefore all the more regrettable that we do not possess further information about the 'plateelbakkers en -schilders' who worked there. The polychrome objects have special characteristics as well, as is exemplified by an octagonal jar with a lid and an open blue, red, green and brown decoration which is spread freely, like composition, across its eight surfaces (*ill. 80*). In a three-part set executed in the Kashmir technique, which consists of a jar with a lid and two gourd vases, also with lids, the artist kept to the decoration of each separate surface; however their ornamentation is particularly distinguished because of the climbing peonies which alternate with hydrangeas (*ill. 75*). We also have, dating from the period during which the Van Dijk family managed the factory, objects for daily use and sets of dishes, which were very popular later when the muffle technique was used. Among others, the artists took as their models the Chinese 'famille verte' porcelain dating from the K'ang-hsi period. Many pieces belonging to one of these tableware sets have been preserved. They may be considered as the *chefs d'oeuvre* of this factory. The dragon motif, the Kylin and the Fong Hoang bird in a landscape form patterns in the centre of the plate; the borders are decorated with braidwork and butterflies. An evenly luminous green predominates among the colours, next to blue, violet, rust-red and yellow. Some plates are signed with the Roos mark (Mark 121).

De Witte Starre (The White Star)

This factory only gained its greatest popularity in 1761 under Albert Kiell. It had been well known in the years after 1700 but the reason for this was mainly its connection with De Roos. This link had been established by Dammas Hofdijk, who managed De Roos from 1694 to 1712 and also was the owner of De Witte Starre after 1705. Characteristic examples of blue Delft faience prove that the same designs were used in both factories (*ills. 54, 55*). Dammas Hofdijk died in 1726 and Jacobus de Lange, the co-owner of De Roos, had transferred to De Witte Starre. Jacobus de Lange died in 1723; after 1726 his widow took over the factory and sold it in 1741. We may assume that a hexagonal blue star was used as the factory mark from 1705 until 1741 (Mark 140). Little is known about later products until 1764 when Albert Kiell had his mark registered (Mark 144). Among polychrome Delft faience, as well as blue, there are objects which show that the workmanship of De Witte Starre was of a high order. The oval octagonal central platter and the eight individual matching dishes make for an odd 'objet de l'époque' (*ill. 77*). A similar dish made by Rochus Hoppesteyn is shown in illustration 65. These sets can be explained by the ladies' tea popular at that time which has been described in discussing the small teapots. The dishes were used to offer a large selection of sweet titbits, pralines and other sweetmeats. It is appropriate that this dish should have been made during the peak period of polychrome Delft faience: that is 1700–30.

Ill. 83. One of two octagonal plaques decorated with a Chinese terrace; 'famille rose' style. No mark, *c.* 1725. Privately owned.

There are very many unsigned works of art, both polychrome and blue, which represent highpoints in technique and painting in the Far Eastern manner. It is not possible to establish even the slightest connection between these objects and any of the well-known Delft factories. This fact demonstrates the extent of our present ignorance of the works of art and even the artists of the Delft industry. Two examples with outstanding figure composition deserve our particular attention. Many more could be provided.

Two large square tea caddies, which are privately owned, represent on each side an open landscape with lovely women and playing children (*ill. 81*). The ornamentation is technically perfect; the plum blossoms permit us to suppose that gold paint was used and an approximation of the Japanese Kakiemon style.

Another example is taken from the Chinese 'famille rose' style, namely, two plaques (*ill. 83*) whose octagonal frame is in perfect harmony with the picture. The terrace decorated with flowers on which a young woman turns to a small boy running towards her is a setting full of light and charm.

Finally a remarkable example should be mentioned which shows how even polychrome faience followed the times. Plaques began to take the place of paintings of flowers. *Illustration 82* provides an appropriate example: it is one of two rare unsigned plaques with a colourful bouquet against a white background. While they are in the tradition of tile paintings, the flower bouquet is already characteristic of the Baroque period. In imitation of the landscape plaques framed in black wood as made by Frijtom, the 'painting' now became a ceramic unit by incorporating the black frame. Unwittingly this brought on a transition to a new technique, the making of black Delft faience, a development which took place around the year 1700.

VIII. Polychrome Delft Faience on Dark Brown, Olive-Green or Black Background. Nevers Blue Faience: 1670—1740

In manufacturing polychrome decorations on dark brown, olive-green and particularly on black backgrounds Delft faience reached a new peak of technical perfection combined with more refined artistic workmanship. (Almost all black faience objects are now either in museums or privately owned and it is very unlikely that new pieces will be discovered.) Only a limited and regrettably incomplete review of the work of artists who made this type of faience can be provided here. The history of the factories might complete the picture, but only in part. We know some of the factories which manufactured these objects, but as in the case of the widespread imitations of the 'famille rose' and the Kakiemon style (*ills. 81, 83*), there are innumerable unsigned black Delft faience plaques the origin of which we cannot guess on the basis of their design.

An oval black plaque depicting a sitting and a standing figure is a unique work. The latter carries a white rabbit in her arms. There is also a vase containing a plum tree branch and a parrot on a tall stand around which a dragon is entwined (Plate XIV). The basic colour is a light emerald-green, which harmonizes well with the reddish-brown and golden-yellow tones and produces light effects which fully bring out the delicate features of the faces. One wonders where the artist found the inspiration for this motif.

Black faience reminds one immediately of the Chinese 'famille noire' or the golden-yellow design on a black background—the so-called 'mirror black'—which also dates from the K'ang-hsi period. Possibly black faience was also influenced by Far Eastern lacquer art, which was generally used after 1700 to decorate the panels of European furniture. The painting technique used on plates and tea caddies among others is particularly reminiscent of lacquer ware. There are also imitations of gold lacquer, multicoloured marble and mother-of-pearl.

A discussion of black Delft faience leads us to consider the factories which practised this art.

De Romeyn (The Roman)

This factory did not play an important part in the development of Delft faience until 1671 when Martinus Gouda and Ary de Milde each bought one half of it. Ary de Milde withdrew after a year but Martinus Gouda (d. 1687) worked in it until 1678, and very likely even longer. He registered a mark in 1680 which shows a resemblance to the six-part signature of the K'ang-hsi porcelain. In the Brussels museum there are three jars, two of which are marked with a similar symbol, so that

Ill. 84. Large jar with Chinese decoration on olive-green background. No mark. Attributed to Martinus Gouda. De Romeyn, 1670–80. Amsterdam, Rijksmuseum.

there is no definite proof that Martinus Gouda really manufactured these objetcs. The Rijksmuseum also owns a similar object (*ill. 84*) without a mark, but of outstanding quality. The picture is drawn in a restrained shade of yellow on an olive-green background; it represents a pagoda with terraces and rocks, a scattered flower pattern in between, birds beating their wings in mid-air and climbing peonies which are in relief. Presumably these objects were among the first to be manufactured in black faience.

Het Jonge Moriaenshooft

Lieven van Dalen came from a family of potters whose members worked in Delft from 1667 to 1730. Two of his sons were employed in other factories, but we do not know any of their works. Three months after Rochus Hoppesteyn's death in 1692 Lieven van Dalen bought Het Jonge Moriaenshooft from his widow. He was an artist who mainly limited himself to making objects for everyday use; we know only one decorative piece by him. The themes he used in his designs are just as limited, but they are of outstandig quality. The drawings are very meticulous and consist mainly of single flowering branches and insects on dark brown or an olive-green background. On the sides of his teapots flowering bushes are rooted in a small clump of earth, but the border decoration is again limited to spirals, criss-crossed lines or arches (*ills. 85, 86, 87*). The surface of an olive-green pot for sampling tea is only large enough for a small scattered flower pattern. It should also be noted that Van Dalen never made any blue or polychrome faience.

Ill. 85. Hexagonal wine jug with Chinese decoration on olive-green background. Mark: LVD (Lieven van Dalen). Het Jonge Moriaen-shooft, 1692–1730. Brussels, Musées royaux d'Art et d'Histoire

Ill. 86. Teapot with Chinese decoration on olive-green background. Mark: LVD (Lieven van Dalen). Het Jonge Moriaenshooft, 1692–1730. Privately owned.

Ill. 87. Small dish with Chinese decoration on brown and olive-green background. Mark: LVD (Lieven van Dalen). Het Jonge Moriaenshooft, 1692–1730. Brussels, Musées royaux d'Art et d'Histoire.

Ill. 88. Teapot with Chinese decoration. Black background. Mark:
PAK (Pieter Adriaenson Kocksz.).
De Grieksche A, 1701–22. Amsterdam, Rijksmuseum.

Ill. 89. So-called 'trembleuse'
chocolate-cup with Chinese decoration. Black background. Mark:
LVE en IEDK (Lambert van Eenhoorn and Eduard de Koningh?).
De Metalen Pot, 1691–1721. Amsterdam, Rijksmuseum.

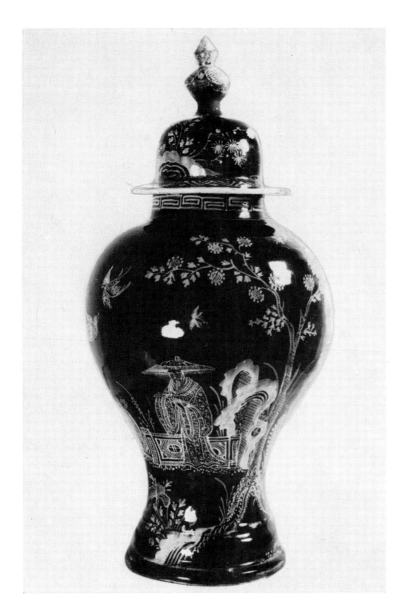

De Grieksche A

This factory also made black faience although it did so by its own special technique. The polychrome flower pattern was applied in blue, red, yellow and grey-green to the white surface which was only then filled in with black, in such a way that a narrow white border under-scores the outline of the picture. We know a number of teapots, dishes for decorating cupboards and fairly large vases with the mark PAK (Pieter Adriaenson Kocks, Mark 61), whose factory mark permits them to be dated between 1700—25. Among the objects for daily use which were unknown until recently, are the 'trembleuses' or chocolate cups with a lid and a deep saucer into which the cup fits. Both De Grieksche A and De Metalen Pot manufactured 'trembleuses'.

Ill. 91. Washbasin and ewer with Chinese decoration on black background. Mark: LVE or LVF (Lambert van Eenhoorn or Louwijs Victorson). De Metalen Pot or De Dobbelde Schenckan, 1691–1721 or 1688–1713. Brussels, Musées royaux d'Art et d'Histoire.

Ill. 92. Plate with Chinese decoration on black background. No mark, *c.* 1700. Privately owned.

Ill. 93. One of two polychrome figures representing
a wine-drinker. Mark: LVE
(Lambert van Eenhorn). De
Metalen Pot, 1691–1721.
Brussels, Musées royaux
d'Art et d'Histoire.

De Metalen Pot and De Dobbelde Schenckan

Without doubt both of these factories can lay claim to having produced the most magnificent black
faience. The confusion about the monograms LVE and LVF permits us to honour both potteries
equally, since there is no indication whatsoever of the factory of origin of objects bearing these
marks.

But before considering these pieces a number of cases, jars and tumblers must be mentioned in
connection with De Metalen Pot. They are signed CK, *i.e.,* Cornelis van der Kloot (Marks 30–32),
who transferred from De Dissel to De Metalen Pot in 1697, in order to 'bevrijden' (release) Lam-

Ill. 94. Teapot with Chinese decoration on black background. Mark: LVE or LVF (Lambert van Eenhoorn or Louwijs Victorson). De Metalen Pot or De Dobbelde Schenckan, 1691–1721 or 1688–1713. London, Victoria and Albert Museum.

Ill. 95. Small oval plaque with Chinese decoration on black background. No mark, *c.* 1700. Privately owned.

Ill. 96. Back of a clothes' brush, ornamentation on black background. No mark, *c.* 1700. The Hague, Gemeente Museum.

bert van Eenhoorn. He was probably the first to manufacture black faience in this factory. His basic type of Chinese-derived decoration points to a relationship with Martinus Gouda. A jar (*ill. 90*), part of a cupboard set consisting of five pieces, is a good example of Van der Kloot's extraordinarily delicate drawing. It is muted yellow, showing figures surrounded by large rocks and slender flowering trees. (In the Brussels museum there are a few dark brown faience objects which are incorrectly attributed to Van der Kloot in Cat. I Pièces Marquées, Ill. 72.)

Plate XVII
Oval polychrome plaque with Chinese decoration.
No mark, *c.* 1730. Privately owned.

The works signed LVE or LVF are choice pieces in the truest sense of the word. The ewer and basin (*ill. 91*) which were used during meals for washing the hands are fine examples. A similar set was made by the silversmith Lutma in Amsterdam on the occasion of the inauguration of the Amsterdam town hall. However, the faience made after 1700 is considerably more delicate in form and rhythm.

Among the black faience of high quality there are also tea caddies, teapots, decorative plates and small figurines which could have been made in either of the factories. A black teapot decorated with a polychrome landscape is attributed to Louwijs Victorson, perhaps rightly so. The two side surfaces show a riverscape with a pagoda and a fishing boat; the remaining space is decorated with the usual flower pattern (*ill. 94*).

Ill. 97. Wine jug with silver lid. Chinese decoration on Nervers blue background. Mark: De Paeuw David Kam, before 1725. Rotterdam, Boymans van Beuningen Museum.

The decorative plates and the tea caddies, whose yellow and green decoration on a black background is reminiscent of Chinese or Japanese lacquer ornamentation, are particularly effective. Some of these objects are signed LVE and others LVF, but there are also plates without any mark (*ill. 92*). One's first reaction would be unhesitatingly to attribute them to one of the two factories under discussion were it not that other, unsigned, pieces with the same motifs but on an olive-green rather than a black background are in museums in London and Brussels. Their style also recalls Lieven van Dalen's speciality and we cannot therefore make a definite attribution of them.

Other painters, whose names we do not know, tried to achieve special affects against a black background by using harsher colours or by trying to give the look of red or green marble to the underside of a plate. As these plates are also unsigned we cannot attribute them to any factory.

A consideration of animal and human figurines again brings us to De Metalen Pot. This pottery had already manufactured such objects in blue faience; the human figures were somewhat humorous in conception but were not very carefully executed, as may be seen in the statuette of the winedrinker (*ill. 93*) where the pedestal displays careless workmanship. Two unsigned figurines of roosters, used as oil and wine containers, are however very effective in the contrast of their bright red and blue-green feathers and golden-yellow necks against the black glaze (*ill. 98*).

Finally two unmarked objects, the origins of which we cannot determine, should be mentioned. Clothes' brushes made of black faience are characteristic of this period (*ill. 96*) as is an oval plaque (*ill. 95*) with a flowing design of plants and birds in a rocky landscape. It is noteworthy that the shiny white flowers come very close to imitating pinkish-blue mother-of-pearl and that the golden-yellow dotted line is reminiscent of gold lacquer.

Ill. 98. Two polychrome roosters on black background. No mark. Attributed to Lambert van Eenhoorn. De Metalen Pot, 1691–1721. Privately owned.

Ill. 99. Very large dish with Chinese flower decoration on dark Nevers blue background. No mark, *c.* 1750 (?). Brussels, Musées royaux d'Art et d'Histoire.

Nevers Blue Faience

After the death of Gerrit Kam and his son Pieter (1705) the family property was divided. De 3 Vergulde Astonnekens became the share of Pieter's daughter, while De Paeuw became the property of David Kam, who died in 1719. The factory passed into other hands after the death of Kam's widow in 1725. David Kam, who was a 'meester plateelbakker', registered the full name of the pottery as its factory mark. He specialized in Nevers blue for backgrounds: a steel-blue or dark blue colouring in the manner of Chinese porcelain, a style which is also called 'bleu persan' (*ill. 97*). His use of this background had a decisive influence on his design, which consists of Chinese flower vines and birds freely spread over the whole surface. The shades vary from cream-coloured to light or greenish-yellow. A very large round dish, decorated on the inside and outside with a scattered design of flowering branches and insects is an odd example of this type of Delft (*ill. 99*). Its shape and size, however, lead one to date it to a later period than Kam's work.

IX. Tile Pictures and Plaques. Rooms Tiled with Blue, Polychrome and Black Delft Faience: 1680—1740

About 1700 the Dutch tile industry was stimulated by French decorative arts to produce tile pictures and plaques to ornament fireplaces and interiors of homes. We know examples of this production, supported by documentary evidence, from Delft and Rotterdam. The bill, dated July 30, 1695, for the dishes ordered for the dairy at Hampton Court Palace as a present from William III to Queen Mary states that 'there is due to Adriaenson Kocks of Delft for Dutch China or ware...' The dairy, 'in which Her Majesty took great delight', was provided with a tiled room the panels of which were decorated with copies of engravings by Daniel Marot. (The order was filled by De Grieksche A which later adopted many of Marot's designs.) Each panel consists of four compositions. Plate XV shows the second from the top with a portrait of the king on horseback. Each tile measured 62 cm. square. King William ordered the dairy to be dismantled in 1698 and neither the tiles nor dishes have been preserved *in situ* at the palace, although some of the other faience does remain there.

Oval plaques with raised frames also became popular as wall decorations. They took the place of the seventeenth-century tiles with landscapes framed in black. One example among many is an oval plaque (Plate XVI) showing a gabled mansion with steps and terraces designed in the style of French chateaux. This plaque is also based on one of Marot's designs.

The polychrome tile pictures decorated with flower vases from a special group. In the Netherlands they were used as ornaments for the back wall of open fireplaces; elsewhere they were used to decorate tiled rooms. Altogether fourteen such tile pictures are presently known. Seven of them are still *in situ,* four in Rambouillet and three in Amalienburg; five are in museums (three in Amsterdam, one in London and one in Sèvres) and two were on the art market in 1965. One of the pictures, now in the Rijksmuseum, came originally from the room of the director of an orphanage in Sommelsdijk, Holland. It was probably put into the wall of the fireplace in 1722. It was copied in 1876 before it was removed and we therefore know how it was originally used. This usage indicates that the tile pictures replaced the vases filled with fresh flowers which, during the seventeenth century, were put into the fireplaces during the summer. All flower-tile pictures are designed in the same way and they were usually thirteen tiles in height and eight in width. They were probably all manufactured in the same factory since they all have the same basic pattern in spite of differences in details. With the exception of a single blue picture (that from Sommelsdijk) they are all polychrome. In eight of the pictures the flower vase stands under an arch which rests on pillars; the six others do not have this framework. In the manner of the

Ill. 100. One of four polychrome tile pictures with a flower vase. No mark. Probably made in the De Roos factory *c.* 1725. Rambouillet castle near Paris.

work of contemporary painters and graphic artists such as Johannes Teyler and Carel Allard, the flower arrangements also include exotic blooms, birds, butterflies and insects as part of the colourful ensemble; in addition one is struck by the rooster and the parrot on either side of the vase which occur in almost all the pictures. We again find an Italian Renaissance motif in the decoration of the arch but in combination with Oriental flowers. Mythological representations alternate with European or Chinese landscapes or gardens in the medallions on the vases. These pictures can be dated from about 1720.

The four tile pictures (*ill. 100*) in the Rambouillet garden hall were installed at the request of the Comte de Toulouse shortly after 1715, certainly before 1730. Probably the idea of using a tiled room as a summer dining room or a garden hall is French in origin. The impetus was probably provided by the Trianon de Porcelaine which Louis XIV had built for Mme de Montespan and which formed part of the royal apartments in the gardens of Versailles from 1670 to 1687. A number of French architects of that period were responsible for the construction and furnishings of many German castles, the court architects of the Bavarian archdukes being examples. They were the architects who designed the hunting pavillion, the summer dining room and the staircases in Brühl, Falkenlust and Nymphenburg.

In Germany only the Amalienburg hunting pavillion in Nymphenburg park will be considered in this connection. Archduke Karl Albrecht of Bavaria had Amalienburg built by the French architect François Cuvilliés; the pavillion was finished in 1734. It was planned as a kitchen in two sections—one for cooking, the other for preparing the food—and next to it a dining room for guests, quite in the spirit of the Arcadian hunting feasts of the Rococo period. Between the two kitchen sections, a wall, which rested on two tile-covered pillars, extended to the ceiling. In the kitchen proper there was sufficient room for movement around the stove; the entrance to the dining room was beyond the two pillars. The octagonal dining room was subdivided struc-

Ill. 102. An attempt, by the use of photographs, to reconstruct the original design of a tile picture in the Amalienburg hunting pavilion.

103   104

104

Ill. 105. View of the kitchen in the Nymphenburg Castle.

Ill. 103. A tile picture in the Amalienburg hunting pavilion. Again, some of these tiles have been incorrectly laid.

Ill. 104. Another attempt to reconstruct by the use of photographs the original design of a tile picture in the Amalienburg hunting pavilion.

turally into tiled walls with pillars and wood panelling. The tiles came from De Bloempot in Rotterdam, owned by the Aelmis family, father and son, who also made the tiles for the tiled rooms in Brühl Castle and the staircase of the Falkenlust hunting pavillion near Brühl (1725–48). Besides three flower-vase pictures on the wall above the kitchen pillars there are in the dining room three other tile paintings—a large one and two small ones—with Chinese motifs in polychrome and black Delft faience (ills. 101–104). It seems likely that these were manufactured in Delft.

Unfortunately errors were made in laying both the flower-vase tiles and the paintings with Chinese motifs. The errors can probably be explained by the fact that after 1725 François Cuvilliés was working on the construction of a new wing for the Residenz palace in Munich and had planned a tiled room as well as halls decorated with tile paintings on the same floor. (This plan was made plain by the existence of a tiled toilet discovered in 1944 when the castle was completely destroyed by bombs.) However the new wing was partially destroyed by fire during its construction in 1729 and there was no further question of decorating it with tiles when it was rebuilt. More than a thousand tiles must have been stored until Cuvilliés found use for them in 1734 in the Amalienburg kitchen. They were laid in 1739, but after a delay of ten years the workers seem to have lacked the patience to assemble each tile painting according to the original design. That is probably how errors which could not be corrected later were made.

A member of the Nymphenburg museum staff has tried to reconstitute the Chinese motifs with the help of photographs. Certain gaps remain however: some tiles are missing and for some others the right spot cannot be found (ills. 101–104). Historically speaking, some observations can be made concerning the Chinese themes on the basis of the picture in Amsterdam which is intact. Altogether there are five such tile pictures, all of which are basically composed in the same manner with only minor differences of detail. The picture reads from top to bottom like a kakemone scroll and should be considered a Dutch variation on a Chinese theme. The Budhisattva Kuwan Yin is enthroned on a lotus flower, aureoled by the sun and scatters 'de zoete dauw der genade' (the sweet dew of grace) over the world. The path, on which there are noblemen and ferociously attired warriors, leads downhill among palaces and tea pavillions. By comparison, the picture in Amalienburg only shows groups of Chinese travelers.

The tile painting in Amsterdam and the Brussels fragment represent Tapuya Indians—unknown until then—based on the drawings and paintings of Albert van Eekhout who accompanied Johan Maurits van Nassau to Brazil (1637–44). The Orange hall in Huis ten Bosch castle was also decorated with drawings of Indians (1648–52). Albert van Eeckhout's work aroused international interest because of presents made to courts abroad. In 1687, the Manufacture des Gobelins in Paris wove a series of wall hangings, called 'Les Indes', based on these drawings; a second series followed in 1737. The Delft faience factories also seized upon this theme and represented Tapuya Indians on their tile paintings.

Where were these flower-vase tiles and scenes from Chinese life manufactured? As far as the flower vases are concerned, De Roos should certainly be considered a possibility; aside from the making of decorative objects special attention was given there to the manufacturing of tiles, particularly while the management of the factory was in the hands of the Van Dijk family (1713–55). Many tile pictures must have been made there as well, since in 1755 mention was

made of a tile-firing plant belonging to it. A gable-stone, in the Museum Het Prinsenhof, Delft, dating from the year 1779, is decorated with a red rose and the inscription 'Tegelbakkerij van de Roos' (De Roos Tile Bakery). There is also a stylistic argument for this assumption: on eight of the fourteen tile pictures known to us, a flower occurs which resembles a snowball or a hydrangea surrounded by a red line and which corresponds to the flowers appearing on a group of vases signed 'Roos'. De Roos, De Witte Starre and De Bloempot (The Flowerpot) in Rotterdam which belonged to the Aelmis family, also worked together and coordinated shipments abroad.

There is, however, no certainty about the factories in which the scenes from Chinese life, made predominantly of black faience, were manufactured. Both De Metalen Pot and De Dobbelde Schenckan are possibilities as each produced important work in black faience. Nor is it possible to make a definite atribution of these vivid and colourful compositions to De Grieksche A in spite of the magnificent blue tiles this factory made for the dairy at Hampton Court. Only their outstanding quality suggests this factory.

Finally a word should be said about the blue and polychrome plaques made in the eighteenth century. They are almost never signed and must therefore be catalogued according to date and quality. As in black faience and in the 'famille rose' style, the highest quality objects were produced until about 1740. A definite regression can be noted after 1750 when the designs became coarser and more farcical. French ornamentation asserts itself both in the Chinese and the European decorations. Plate XVII and *illustration 106* are typical examples of a mixture of both styles. Polychrome plaques with 'famille verte', Imari and European elements can claim an outstanding place as works of art particularly because of the very delicate workmanship of the border motifs. The polychrome plaque with the three flower vases is wholly due to the influence of French pottery and its strange, asymmetrical decorations can be traced back to French rococo.

X. Polychrome Delft Faience Fired at Low Temperatures: 1680–1750

Even before 1700 Rochus Hoppesteyn, together with Jeremias Godtling in The Hague, learned to decorate faience with fire-resistant red and gold colours and they managed to preserve the secret of their technique. A process whereby these colours could be fixed was discovered and generally used only later when trade relations had been established between the Netherlands and Japan. By that time Japan had a flourishing porcelain industry which was competitive with China—a development due mainly to the efforts of two Japanese, Sakaido Kakiemon and Higashyima Tokyemon, who had learned the art of manufacturing porcelain in China.

The arrival in the Netherlands of Imari porcelain (the name refers to the port from which it was shipped) led various Delft factories to attempt, shortly after 1700, to imitate it. Successful emulation was possible only with the use of the muffle kiln (see Chapter I). With this technique, once the high-temperature dark blue decoration on a white background had been fired, lacquer or rust-red and gold decorations were applied and the ware was fired again at a lower temperature in the muffle kiln.

At first the Imari style, with its dense red or golden flower patterns, (*ills. 107, 108*) was simply copied, but soon a looser composition with Far Eastern and European motifs was developed. Imari-style faience decorated with bright blue, red, green and gilding became very popular although blue and polychrome faience fired at high temperatures retained their appeal. The result was an enrichment of the colour spectrum with bright colours, the opening of new markets and an increased ability to compete with European ceramics. In short, the new technique brought new achievement and a greater reputation to Delft.

Only a few Delft factories used the muffle technique and we will consider three of these.

De Grieksche A (1701–22)

Under the direction of Pieter Adriaenson Kocks and his wife Johanna van der Heul this factory acquired a well-deserved reputation for its Imari-style faience. Dr H. E. van Gelder's research has revealed that in 1713 Johanna contracted with three 'goutschilders' (painters in gold) to 'specialyck de konst van het gout te schildren en te backen op het Delfts porceleyn te oefenen' (exercise in particular the art of painting and firing Delft porcelain with gold). We know the work of only one of these artists because of the monogram AR (Mark 6) which stands for Ary

Ill. 107. Polychrome twelve-sided dish. Imari style. No mark, first half of the 18th century. Arnhem, Gemeente Museum.

Ill. 108. Polychrome teapot. Imari style. Mark: PAK (Pieter Adriaenson Kocks). De Grieksche A, 1701–1722. The Hague, Gemeente Museum.

Ill. 109. Two polychrome sconces with the coat of arms of Frederick 1 of Prussia, European Imari style. Mark: PAK (Pieter Adriaenson Kocks). De Grieksche A, before 1713. Rotterdam, Boymans van Beuningen Museum.

Ill. 110. Polychrome inkwell. European Imari style. Mark: PAK (Pieter Adriaenson Kocks). De Grieksche A, 1701–1722. Brussels, Musées royaux d'Art et d'Histoire.

Ill. 111. Polychrome beer jug. Imari style. Pewter lid. Mark: PAK (Pieter Adriaenson Kocks). De Grieksche A, 1701–1722. Privately owned.

van Rijsselberg who was employed by De Grieksche A until 1718. (All the objects fired in the muffle kiln at this factory are signed with the factory mark PAK—*i.e.,* Pieter Adriaenson Kocks.) Van Rijsselberg, a 'meester goutschilder', moved in 1718 to De 3 Vergulde Astonnekens which had been managed since 1712 by Zacharias Dextra. (Dextra became its owner in 1721 and directed the factory until 1757.) We may assume that while at De Grieksche A Van Rijsselberg signed those objects which he made and claimed them as his own.

Numerous objects for everyday use made of Imari-style faience were also designed for ornamental purposes. Many examples have been preserved. It became very fashionable to order sets of dishes and household utensils such as beer jugs, vases, teapots, tea caddies, inkwells and flowerpots and, not

Plate XVIII
Two octagonal polychrome salt-cellars, Kakiemon
style. No mark. Attributed to Ary van Rijsselberg, 1718—35. The Hague, Gemeente Museum.

Ill. 112. Polychrome octagonal vase with gilt decoration. Mark: PAK (Pieter Adriaenson Kocks). Attributed to Ary van Rijsselberg. De Grieksche A, 1713–1718. Privately owned.

least, plates painted with the family coat of arms decorated with gold. This type of faience became internationally known and many shipments abroad were made. The most famous export is probably the set of dishes made for Frederick III, archduke of Brandenburg who in 1701 became King Frederick I of Prussia. The set was decorated with a crowned coat of arms, the insignias of the Order of the Black Eagle—in which the Eagle of Brandenburg and the Eagle of Prussia alternate—and the crowned monogram F(edericus R(ex). Almost all the dishes are signed PAK and must therefore have been painted by one of the artists working in gold at De Grieksche A (*ill. 109*).

De Dobbelde Schenckan (1713–35)

As far as faience fired at low temperatures is concerned, only a brief remark need be made about this factory.

It can be stated with certainty that Victor Louwijson did not have any Imari-style faience made. His son-in-law, Jacob van Thiel, succeeded him in the factory. We have little information about him to date, but we do know that even before 1721 two painters, Gilles and Hendrick de Koningh, worked in De Dobbelde Schenckan and made objects in the Imari style. In 1735, after Jacob van Thiel's death, they bought the factory in their capacity as trustees of young Hendrick de Koningh Jr. Their ward attained his legal majority by getting married and was then dubbed 'meester porceleynbacker'. Two small flowerpots, with the mark GDK and HDK and the year 1721 (*ill. 107*, Mark 133) will indicate their style. The medallions are decorated with green, red, violet and gold animals, birds and flowers, while the blue borders have a design of golden arabesques. The two pots represent an elegant although modest contribution to the Imari style. Eduard de Koningh, one of the painters working in gold, also belonged to this family of potters; he made a contract with Johanna van der Heul in 1713 and then worked at De Grieksche A.

Ill. 114. Polychrome plate with gilt decoration. Mark: AR (Ary van Rijsselberg). De 3 Vergulde Astonnekens, 1718–1735. Privately owned.

Ill. 115. Polychrome plate with group of horsemen, 'famille verte' style. Mark: AR (Ary van Rijsselberg). De 3 Vergulde Astonnekens, 1718–1735. Brussels, Musées royaux d'Art et d'Histoire.

De 3 Vergulde Astonnekens (1712—57)

It is only very rarely that one can follow in detail the development of the work of an artist. One such artist is Frederik van Frijtom; another is Ary van Rijsselberg during the years 1718—1735, although we must rely on suppositions for the period during which he worked at De Grieksche A. Thus, for example, we cannot be certain in attributing to him an octagonal vase over which bright red and light green vines are scattered (*ill. 112*). It is an object of outstanding beauty, but it is signed PAK (Pieter Adriaenson Kocks). There are similar borderline cases of stylistically related objects, such as the inkwell with reddish-blue and gold Imari decorations marked PAK (*ill. 110*) and the large flowerpot with handles which is signed with the initials AR (Musées royaux d'Art et d'Histoire, Brussels). Three plates signed AR (*ills. 113—15*) show plainly the versatility of his talent, developed by his understanding of Chinese and Japanese models. In contrast to the forceful, bright Imari colours on a dark blue background, he decorated his medallions with very precise Kakiemon style drawings of small hedges of woven reeds, lovely birds and delicate vines. His preference for red and green can be seen on a plate decorated with the strong flowering branches of a plum tree from which a parrot greedily watches his insect prey (*ill. 114*). In this instance, he abandoned completely the Japanese style in order to turn to an imitation of the Chinese 'famille verte' style. The plate representing a group of horsemen (*ill. 115*) decorated altogether in the 'famille verte' style proves how much more refined his style became (1723—35). We know several similar plates, some with minor modifications in the posture and the number of figures. The group depicted here probably represents a delegation sent to deliver an invitation to Confucius on behalf of the duke of Lu. The faience is exceptionally thin and can hardly be distinguished from porcelain. The manner of the drawing has become purely narrative and eschews the surroundings. The figures are full of life and movement, they are emphasized by a thin dark outline to contrast the colours with each other. Turquoise is the predominant colour next to red, violet, blue, pink, yellowish-brown and gold. The border, decorated in European Régence style, is also noteworthy; it had already appeared in Rijsselberg's blue faience about 1730. After what has been said of his skills, it may not be too bold to attribute to the work of his later years two polychrome unsigned salt-cellar perfect in design, technique and colours of blue, turquoise, red and gold in the pure Kakiemon style. We can undoubtedly assume that they were made by one of the best artists of the period working in gold (Plate XVIII).

Ill. 117. Polychrome oval tureen with lid and saucer, European decoration. Mark: Z. Dextra. De 3 Vergulde Astonnekens, 1712–57. Privately owned.

Ill. 118. Small butter dish with lid, Kakiemon decoration. No mark, first part of the 18th century. Arnhem, Gemeente Museum.

Ills. 119 and 120. Two polychrome tiles. Kakiemon and 'famille rose' decoration. No mark. Delft, first part of the 18th century. Privately owned.

Meanwhile the owner of the factory began to fire faience according to the muffle technique, but the objects themselves as well as the decoration were modelled mainly on German porcelain. It was only exceptionally (1736—95) that objects were made with 'famille rose' decoration which was sometimes completed by small flower branches. Among them were mainly small lidded tureens, butter dishes and barber's basins. Among the unsigned pieces which we know are an armorial plate, a child's dish, a view of the sea or a historical event like the taking of the city of Maastricht by the Prince of Parma in 1759, based on an engraving of Jan Luyken. In this case, however, the quality of the objects indicates clearly that the best period of Delft faience fired at low temperatures had already passed.

Zacharias Dextra managed the factory until 1757 and used the mark 'Z. Dex.', to which 'De 3 astonne' (Marks 4, 5) was sometimes added. We do not know the names of the artists who worked in gold. A tureen (*ill. 117*) is a typical mixture of the European style. The oval medallions represent Dutch riverscapes with sailing ships similar to those which appear on tiles. On the river bank there is a forest, an imaginary church, a city gate and fashionably dressed burghers. We can date the tureen from the middle of the eighteenth century.

Unsigned pieces made with the muffle-kiln technique are frequently of particularly good quality. This is true of a butter dish (*ill. 118*) which is decorated delicately in the Kakiemon style. The charming flower baskets depicted on this piece do not yield in quality to the polychrome salt-cellars (cf. Plate XVIII). Topping off the lid with a gilt calf is a typically Dutch note.

Belonging to the same category of muffle-fired objects are the polychrome tiles manufactured in

Delft (*ills. 119, 120*). The Kakiemon decoration consists of delicate flower baskets with handles painted blue, violet, green, red and gold in a round medallion. The corners are filled in with cross-hatched leaves or with a rose motif. A second basic design used on these tiles comprises a sturdily woven basket completely filled with flowers; however this is more reminiscent of the 'famille rose' decoration. At the same time, or perhaps a little later, tiles decorated with ships were made in this style, although they were of somewhat inferior quality. It is most likely that the tiles were manufactured in De Roos, which prospered during the first part of the eighteenth century under the management of the Van Dijk family, but we have no proof that faience was fired at low temperatures in this factory. The problem therefore remains unsolved.

XI. Blue and Polychrome Delft Faience Fired at High Temperatures after 1730

The closing of the factories

After 1730 new artists were able to profit from the study of the splendid and varied works of art which had been produced during the fifty preceding years. But Delft faience changed in this later period and the changes became gradually more evident. Thus, although there was almost no change in the techniques, as the demand for household objects increased the artistic qualities of the faience suffered. Quantity surpassed quality: there was what might almost be called mass production.

There was outward prosperity in the Delft industry for about twenty years after 1730 but this prosperity in fact merely concealed the grave problems which confronted the industry. The invention of genuine European porcelain in Saxony and of English creamware created new competitors. These rival wares also influenced the shaping of Delft faience since there was no way of avoiding a certain artistic conformity. Initially the glorious tradition of Delft ware enabled it to hold its own competitively but by about 1750 the Delft potteries were in economic trouble. Some factories survived for quite some time; others declined rapidly and the years 1770–1807 in particular saw the closing of many potteries.

De 3 Vergulde Astonnekens (1730–1807)

Three pieces dating from Ary van Rijsselberg's last years (he died in 1735) demonstrate his versatility. A blue plate (*ill. 124*) represents, almost as if it were a snapshot, a struggle between a dragon and a fox. Every superfluous detail has been omitted; the border design is almost identical with that used for the group of horsemen (*ill. 115*). By contrast, two cows (*ill. 122*) decorated with polychrome flower vines reflect the Dutch character of his work. The making of animal figurines of this type was particularly common in the eighteenth century. These objects bear the initials VR, as distinguished from the monogram AR which we know from other pieces, but we can safely consider VR to stand for Van Rijsselberg.

The factory's last important owner, Hendrick van Hoorn (Marks 7–9), was typical of the new era. No work of art can be attributed to him. He was a 'meester plateelbakker' and from 1777 to 1783 also the owner of De Roos, although details of this ownership are not known. He died in 1803 and left the factory, which was to be managed by his daughter Johanna Catharina, to his children.

Ill. 121. Oval polychrome fruit dish with openwork ornamentation and yellow background. Mark: H: V: H: (Hendrick van Hoorn). De 3 Vergulde Astonnekens, 1757–1803. Amsterdam, Rijksmuseum.

Ill. 122. Two polychrome cows. Mark: VR (Van Rijsselberg). De 3 Vergulde Astonnekens, 1718–35. Privately owned.

121

Ill. 123. Octagonal blue bowl. Chinese decoration. Mark: JB (Justus Brouwer). De Porceleyne Bijl, 1739–1775. Brussels, Musées royaux d'Art et d'Histoire.

Ill. 124. Blue plate with dragon and fox. Mark: AR (Ary van Rijsselberg). De 3 Vergulde Astonnekens, 1718–35. Privately owned.

Ill. 125. Two polychrome sauce-boats with lids and saucers. The lids represent soles and each has a handle in the shape of a prawn. Mark: A hatchet (Justus Brouwer). De Porceleyne Bijl, 1739–1775. Privately owned.

Ill. 126. Polychrome candlestick, one of a pair, with a tree trunk and two seated figures. Mark: HB (Hugo Brouwer). De Porceleyne Bijl or De Drye Porceleyne Flesschen, 1760–1777 or 1788. Brussels, Musées royaux d'Art et d'Histoire.

She, however, sold the factory in the same year although she 'de behandeling der fabriek heeft angeleerd' (had learned to handle the business). In 1807 a house was sold 'voorheen geweest zijnde een plateelbakkerij "de 3 vergulde astonnekens"' (which had previously been the factory De 3 Vergulde Astonnekens).

The pieces signed with Van Hoorn's mark are characteristic of late faience. They consist of the simple blue and polychrome objects for everyday use which were in great demand: for example the polychrome fruit dish with yellow background and open-work ornamentation (*ill. 121*). We also know a few 'mille fleurs' plates with the initials H:V:H:. (Such a design was originally typical of De Dissel but similar products were also made, until 1750, by De Grieksche A after it had taken over the inventory.) If these plates were made in De Roos or De 3 Vergulde Astonnekens Van Hoorn must have owned the designs, as was the case with several other designs.

The inventory of Van Hoorn's estate shows that he must also have made many figurines and animal-shaped objects, the latter of which often were used as pastry or butter dishes. The inventory lists the following: '2 beerenlijders, 2 konijnen, 2 kievitteb, 4 hennen, 1 schaap, 8 eieren' and '5 beelden sijnde Hugo de Groot' (2 bear-baiters, 2 rabbits, 2 lapwings, 4 hens, 1 sheep, 8 eggs and 5 figurines representing Hugo the Great).

De Vergulde Blompot (The Golden Flowerpot) *(1654—1841)*

After its establishment in 1654, this factory unquestionably made a great contribution to the development of Delft faience. A number of well-known names are mentioned in records and contracts concerning, for example, obligations with respect to De Porceleyne Schotel which was next door to De Vergulde Blompot. It is however not possible to relate the incomplete data of the archives to the factory's production, since a factory mark with the initials BP is known only from the year 1734 on. In 1764, the mark 'De Blompot' in cursive writing was registered (Marks 10—12). De Vergulde Blompot was sold several times before Pieter Verburgh became its manager in 1734. In 1756 he also became its owner. He died in 1789.

A teaplant in a meadow on blue Delft faience gives conclusive evidence of careful execution and moreover was a new motif for the period (*post* 1750). The plant fans out in splendid blooms above three chalice-like leaves (*ill. 127*). The same motif was also used at De Grieksche A, although in a different style. About 1750, hundreds of so-called peacock plates were produced in polychrome faience. For a long time after they were copied by various factories. However, characteristically of the coarsening of the faience, the composition gradually grew rigid and the quality of the workmanship poorer. Among the factories which did credit to the original design (*ill. 128*) were:

Ill. 128. So-called peacock plate, polychrome. Mark: A claw and LS (Lambertus Sanderus). De Claeuw, 1764—1806. Leeuwarden, Het Princessehof Museum.

Ill. 129. Small polychrome tea caddy with brown and yellow Chinese decoration. Mark: A claw. De Claeuw, after 1730—64. Arnhem, Gemeente Museum.

De Porceleyne Bijl (The Porcelain Axe) *(1657—1788)* and *De Drye Porceleyne Flesschen* (The Three Porcelain Bottles) *(1661—1777)*

After an early history which is but partially known, these two factories came to the fore about 1740 when they became the family property of Brouwer, father and son. Justus Brouwer (d. 1775) bought De Porceleyne Bijl in 1739 from Jacob Mes. In 1760 he bought De Drye Porceleyne Flesschen for his son Hugo who became first its manager and later, in 1767, its co-owner. Hugo Brouwer signed his work with his initials HB. In 1764 a hatchet was registered as the factory mark (Marks 16—19). He sold De Drye Porceleyne Flesschen in 1777, De Porceleyne Bijl in 1788.

In the field of blue faience, an octagonal bowl signed JB (Mark 15), can be attributed to Justus Brouwer. It is still decorated very much in the K'ang-hsi style, even though some details, in particular the cloudy border, indicate that that tradition no longer had as much influence as in earlier times (*ill. 123*). In addition, it can also be assumed that the best pieces signed with a hatchet are his since Hugo Brouwer developed a more decorative style in his work and, being a member of the younger generation, had a greater part in the production of the faience of the later years, which came closer to being folk art. We may consider two sauce-boats, perfect in moulding and decoration, as part of this group: the lids consist of soles, true to nature in shape and colouring, each of which has a prawn for a handle (*ill. 125*). Hugo Brouwer's work shows a preference for small jugs, flowerpots, French rococo style groups of vases, as well as for human and animal figurines. The first-mentioned faience is executed in blue, manganese or polychrome but because of its coarser shape it has little artistic value.

By contrast, the small figurines led to a new development which in a sense gave Delft faience a meaning and an independence which it retained until the end. The animal figures are simple and realistic, the human figures of Saxon porcelain were, so to speak, translated into Delft faience and had a refining influence on its colour and shaping. Several candlesticks bearing the initials of Hugo Brouwer and therefore probably made by him are very imaginative in form. They have either one or two tree trunks as candleholders with two or three figures sitting under them. Each figure holds on its lap a box with a lid that can be snapped open. The clothing and hair style of the women and the pattern of the dress materials vary. This could only be the work of a very able painter and is at the same time also an example of polychrome faience of the best period (*ill. 126*).

De Porceleyne Claeuw (1658–1840)

Before 1658, a certain Arent Gouda took care of the interests of De Porceleyne Claeuw; only in 1661 was it established 'in compagnieschap', *i.e.,* as the family property of Cornelia, Maria and Elisabeth van Schoonhoven who were registered as 'platielbacksters' and who lived in the house connected with the factory. Cornelia died in 1671, Maria in 1701; Elisabeth sold the factory in 1705 and

Ill. 130. One of three big plates with Chinese decoration. Mark: IHL (Jacobus Harlees). De Porceleyne Fles, 1771–1804. NV Koninkligke Delftsch-Aardewerkfabriek 'De Porceleyne Fles'.

she herself died in 1711. The factory mark in those years was a claw with the initials CVS (Mark 20) which could possibly also stand for Cornelis van Schagen who worked there as 'plateelschilder' (cf. page 152 for the misinterpretation of the capitals LVS for Liesbeth van Schoonhoven, Marks 146, 147). Later the mark consisted only of an irregular drawing of the claw, until Lambertus Sanderus became the factory's owner in 1763 and registered a stylized claw as its mark in 1764 (Marks 21—25). All objects otherwise marked must therefore be dated from before 1764. As for the period between 1705 and 1763, names such as Hendrick Knijff, a 'plateelschilder' in De Metalen Pot in the year 1719 (d. 1729, Mark 109), and Cornelis van Dijk, who was the owner of De Roos from 1739 to 1755, point to connections with other factories.

Besides the peacock plates, the pelican plates also form part of the blue faience manufactured in this factory. In making them, Lambertus Sanderus reverted to the 'Kaapsche Schotels' of the

Plate XIX
Blue chocolate-pot and warmer with landscape
decoration. Mark: GVS (Geertruy Verstelle). Het
Oude Moriaenshooft, 1761–69. Amsterdam, Rijksmuseum.

Plate XX
One of two jars made to match a group of Chinese
vases. Mark: AP (Anthony Pennis). De Twee
Scheepjes 1759–1782 (On the art market in 1965.)

period around 1700, with their porcelain-type character and their violet, grey and blue colouration. Sanderus, however, adapted those models to the style of his own times.

It should be mentioned that one of the 'plateelschilders' of De Porceleyne Claeuw had his own distinctive style. We know some tea caddies with Chinese decoration depicting slender weeping willows (*ill. 129*). The yellow and brown colour combination differs completely from the colours usual in Delft faience. It is not known where this colour style originated.

Ill. 132. Polychrome candlestick with flower decoration. Mark: J: H: F: 1185 (Johan Hermen Frerkingh). 't Fortuyn, 1775–1791. Brussels, Musées royaux d'Art et d'Histoire.

Ill. 133. A pair of polychrome candlesticks, European decoration. Mark: A and JH (De Grieksche A and Jacobus Halder). De Grieksche A, 1764–1768. Arnhem, Gemeente Museum.

Ill. 134. Blue octagonal bread basket or fruit dish with Chinese decoration. Mark: A.D. De Grieksche A, 1758–1764. Amsterdam, Rijksmuseum.

Ill. 135. Plate with blue scattered flower pattern and gold dots. Mark: A and JH (De Grieksche A and Jacobus Halder). De Grieksche A, 1764–1768. Arnhem, Gemeente Museum.

Ill. 136. Blue octagonal dish with régence decoration. Mark: H: VMD (Hendrik van Middeldijk). t' Hart, after 1762. Arnhem, Gemeente Museum.

De Porceleyne Fles (1653 to late eighteenth century)

From the very beginning much could have been expected of this factory under the ownership of Wouter van Eenhoorn and Quirijn van Cleynhoven. Such expectations were fulfilled by Johannes Knotter in 1697–1701 and later by Christoffel and Pieter van Doorne in 1750–71. (Unfortunately some of the records have been lost and we have little information about the years between Knotter and the Van Doornes.) In 1771 Jacobus van Harlees took over the factory and was succeeded by his son Dirck in 1786. Both father and son brought about a curious late-flowering of blue faience.

In the factory's collection, which still exists, there are three plates with Chinese decoration; strangely the decoration spreads beyond the border, the colour being a striking dark blue (*ill. 130*). They added a bottle to their monogram as had Johannes Knotter (Marks 34, 36, 38–40). The Evenepoel collection in the Brussels museum contains two valuable plates with portraits of Roman emperors and a Dutch landscape in the background. It presumably belonged to a group of ten plates. There are also a small royal-blue pot and dish for strawberries with a saucer decorated with yellow and manganese flowers on a turquoise-green background (Cat. Pièces marquées, Coll. Ev. 533). Pieces of this colouration were not usually signed, but because of the existence of these marked objects we can identify with certainty one of the factories which towards the end of the eighteenth century was manufacturing them.

't Fortuyn (Fortune) (1661—1791)

The data available about this factory are sketchy. The records which have been preserved are of an administrative nature and must therefore date from 1750 or later. 't Fortuyn was founded in 1661 and remained, until 1724, the property of the Mes (sch) family with the exception of the years 1691—94 when it was owned by Dammas Hofdijk and Jacobus de Lange. According to a note dating from 1692 Hendrick Peridon worked in 't Fortuyn at that time; in 1702, however, he transferred to De Metalen Pot.

A butter dish with saucer and lid in late régence style is notable for its careful shaping and

Ill. 138. Polychrome coffee-pot with European decoration. Mark: A and JH (De Grieksche A and Jacobus Halder). De Grieksche A, 1764—1768. Leeuwarden, Het Princessehof Museum.

Ill. 139. Group of three small polychrome vases, with two tumblers. Mark: DPkan. De Porceleyne Lampetkan, 1756–1778. Privately owned.

Ill. 140. Polychrome container for spices or toiletries, with lid. European decoration. Mark: G: V: S: (Geertruy Verstelle). Het Oude Moriaenshooft, 1761–69. Privately owned.

balanced pattern (*ill. 131*). During the late period of faience, when Pieter van den Briel and his wife were its owners, 't Fortuyn was among the factories which turned to mass production. Pieter's widow inherited the factory in 1761 and thereafter signed with the letters WVDB (Widow Van den

Ill. 141. Large blue bowl representing the parable of the prodigal son. Mark: JVH (Johannes Verhagen). De Paeuw, 1730. Privately owned.

Ill. 142. Polychrome figure of a cow and milkmaid. Mark: AP (Anthony Pennis). De Twee Scheepjes, 1759–1782. Arnhem, Gemeente Museum.

Briel). In 1769 she sold the factory to Anthony Frerkingh. Johan Herman Frerkingh had worked in the factory from 1762 producing polychrome marked objects (*ill. 132*). He acted as business manager and must also have been a co-owner of the factory. (For factory marks see Marks 46—51).

Ill. 143. Blue candle-stick. Kakiemon design. Mark: VDuyn (Johannes van Duyn). De Porceleyne Schotel, 1763—77. Arnhem, Gemeente Museum.

Ill. 144. Polychrome oval fruit dish with saucer. Flower design on yellow background. Mark: VDuyn (Johannes van Duyn). De Porceleyne Schotel, 1763—77. Brussels, Musées royaux d'Art et d'Histoire.

De Grieksche A (from 1722 until after 1818)

On June 30, 1722, the factory became the property of the Van der Kool-Van der Willigen family. In 1758 the business became the property of their son-in-law Jan Theunis Dextra and his wife Catharina van der Kool and 1764 it was sold to Jacobus Adriaenson Halder. For years the pottery occupied an important place in the Delft faience industry, but although we know the owners' names, we do not know those of the artists who worked there. We do know an inventory dating from the year 1758 which indicates a 'rijke nalatenschap [van] Porceleyngoed' (rich heritage of porcelain) consisting of 'in honderden en duizenden stuks, zowel sier-Delfts o. a. Oost-Indische borden, dierplastiek: hanen, koeien en paarden … 2,133 dosijn gepaard theegoed, blaede van kleerborstels, olieen azijn nesjes, aerbeitesjes en schotels, 120 quisquedoors etc.' (hundreds, even thousands of single pieces of decorative faience like East Indian plates, animal figurines: roosters, cows and horses, and household objects, such as 2133 dozen matching tea sets, backs of clothes' brushes, oil and vinegar cruets, strawberry dishes with saucers, 120 cuspidors, etc.).

Despite this seeming prosperity Jan Theunis Dextra expressed his concern about changing times in a document dated December 16, 1757. There were widespread 'negotie so binne—als buitenlands' (domestic and foreign business connections) and large stocks but: 'zeer weinig lieden bereid gevonden worden tot 't overnemen van zoodanige fabriek en negotie…' (only few persons are willing to take over a factory or to make business connections). When Jan Theunis Dextra registered his marks—an A with a D beneath it or his initials ITD (Marks 65—67)—it was specifically noted that his monogram could only be painted 'onder sijn beste goederen' (beneath his best products), therefore presumably beneath his own works of art, while a D was sufficient for the work of the persons employed by him. It is a fact that the Delft 'nieuwe stijl' developed and prospered when the Dextra family owned the factory. De Grieksche A frequently based itself on European designs, as is proven for instance by the blue bread basket (*ill. 134*) which was made, according to a silver model, in French rococo style. Yet the ornamentation with Wan Li borders points to the 'Kaapsche Schotels', such as the ones made before 1700. (Lambertus Sanderus also made use of these motifs again.) The mark on the bread basket reads A—D; the piece was therefore made by one of the painters in his factory. The rooster in the Rijksmuseum (*ill. 137*) must be considered among his own 'beste goederen' as it has the mark ITD. On December 19, 1764, Jan Theunis Dextra sold De Grieksche A to Jacobus Adriaenson Halder, who continued to manage it until 1768. A and JH was the registered mark (Marks 68—71). It would seem that he used the muffle kiln once more: a plate (*ill. 135*) with a blue scattered flower pattern is decorated with golden dots underneath the glaze. The inventory of the estate of Cornelia van der Kool—van der Willigen, Dextra's sister-in-law, also mentions 'een stel van vijf stucks met gout' (a group, consisting of five pieces, with gold). The polychrome household utensils imitate the European rococo style, and in particular German models (*ills. 133, 138*). Under the management of Jacobus Halder's successor, Jan van den Briel, who was the owner of De Grieksche A in 1768—85, the quality of the products declined noticeably, so that this renowned factory became less and less important (Mark 72).

Ill. 145. Large sconce, blue, with candle holder. Mark: CB with a hexagonal star (Cornelis Janson Brouwer). De Witte Starre, 1723 till 1741. Brussels, Musées royaux d'Art et d'Histoire.

Since they were apparently very successful, several of the factories which were less well known in earlier times should be given full recognition because of their contribution to the manufacture of faience after 1750. Among them were:

't Hart (The Heart) (from 1661 until after 1764) *and De Drye Clocken* (The Three Wooden Shoes) (1670—1840).

These factories can be mentioned together since both were managed by the Mesch family until 1745 and 1725 respectively. Because of Jan van der Laan, father and son (or perhaps one and

138

Ill. 146. Polychrome butter dish with lid and saucer. Mark: A:K and a hexagonal star (Albertus Kiell). De Witte Starre, 1761–1772. (On the art market in 1965.)

Ill. 147. A pair of polychrome ladies' shoes. No mark, *c.* 1750. Privately owned.

the same person?) 't Hart contributed to the development of Delft faience, although we do not have any details about its later phase (factory Marks 74—78). The factory was bought by Hendrik van Middeldijk in 1762 who registered his initials H. VMD set in an oval frame as the factory mark (1764, Mark 78). His work is unassuming and has no personal style. It consists mainly of dishes and objects for everyday use (*ill. 136*) which are sparingly provided with Chinese or European decorations. It is likely that the factory was closed down soon after because of the poor economic conditions of the years which followed.

After 1675, Jan van der Laan worked as 'plateelbakker' in De Drye Clocken. In 1706 a very simple mark—consisting of three bells—was used which was made to stand out more clearly after 1725 by drawing it in relief. In 1764 the initials WVD were registered as the mark of Willem van der Does (Marks 79—84) whose father, Ariaen van der Does, bought the factory from the Mesch family; the year of the transaction is not known. The faience made in De Drye Clocken was in the mode popular after 1750. Many blue and polychrome peacock plates were produced (see page 125) which in fact demonstrate a rigid formalism and the deterioration of worksmanship. The colours used are dark blue, orange and brown. They are reminiscent of early majolica ware, a style still retained in the northern part of the country because of a peasant tradition whereby empty stables were decorated with brightly coloured plates.

The coarse peasant earthenware now managed to find its way as a folk craft into the Delft factories, where—just as had tile manufacturing since the seventeenth century—it still had good prospects.

De Porceleyne Lampetkan (The Porcelain Ewer) *(1637—1811)*

From 1637 to 1703—the transition period from majolica to Delft faience—De Lampetkan was the property of a family of potters, later established in Rotterdam, called Valckenhoff and Van Straten (Verstraten, also known as De la Rue from Haarlem). To date we know none of their faience, just as we do not know any of the pieces made in the years 1703—23 during which De Lampetkan was managed by the Van der Voorn family. Only after May 27, 1723, when Abraham van der Ceel took over the 'geabandonneerde boedel' (abandoned property) of Johan van der Voorn, is there information about the production of De Proceleyne Lampetkan. The members of the Van der Ceel family themselves worked in the factory and at first signed with the factory name—'Lpkan'. Later they used the capital letters LPK, which enables us now to distinguish between four different periods. At first, the factory was managed by Abraham van der Ceel (d. 1741), who left it to his son Maarten (d. 1756). The latter's widow contracted a second marriage with Gerard Brouwer who became the owner from 1756—78, after which a grandchild, Abraham van der Ceel Jr (d. 1810) took over the management of the business (Marks 85—90).

All the objects dating from this period, whether blue or polychrome, were executed in late eighteenth-century style. They consist mainly of decorative pots, sauce-boats, bread baskets, candlesticks, fruit dishes, etc. We know, therefore, that objects for everyday use, from purely decorative

Ill. 148. A pair of polychrome standing figures. No mark. After 1750. Privately owned.

small sets of dishes to ornamental cupboard tops which were suited to delicate rococo furniture, were still being manufactured. The light yellow and manganese coloured landscape or flower decorations framed by a border designed to look like a relief were covered with a greenish-white glaze (*ill. 139*).

Het Oude Moriaenshooft (The Old Moor's Head) *(1761—93)*

In 1761 this factory became the property of Geertruy Verstelle, a 'plateelbackster' who managed it independently until 1769. It may be said of her that she raised Delft ware to standards comparable to what it had enjoyed nearly a century before under the Hoppesteyns of Het Jonge Moriaenshooft. The blue chocolate-pot and warmer (Plate XIX) are solid pieces in the style of German rococo silver; the polychrome container for spices (*ill. 140*), which may have been used for toiletries, shows her originality and dexterity. She used delicate colours to paint a peasant

family and its cattle on the lid, a shepherd and shepherdess in an open landscape on the side, and two angels sounding trumpets on the front. This was all in the Arcadian manner of her time. She signed with the initials G:V:S: (Mark 97).

In 1769 she married Cornelison Janson Fonteyn, the owner of Het Jonge Moriaenshooft. Fonteyn died in 1782 and his brother Thomas became owner of both factories. He sold them in 1792. In the next year it is recorded that both were converted into distilleries.

De Paeuw (1725–71)

In about 1725 Johannes Verhagen (Mark 104) bought De Paeuw from the family of David Kam, who had died in 1719. Verhagen's blue faience seems to have been based on old Dutch engravings, with Biblical subjects (*ill. 141*) or representations of landscapes and scenes from country life in the manner of David Vinckeboons. We know large decorative plates dating from the years 1725, 1728, 1729 and 1730.

After Verhagen's death in 1740 the factory was bought by Jacobus de Milde who began to sign his pieces IDM 1740 (Mark 105). In 1764, however, the mark 'de paeuw' was registered. Jacobus's son Abraham was named business manager in 1772 but by 1779 the factory appears to have been closed.

Ill. 150. Syrup pitcher with handle. The cartouche bears the inscription: S(iroop) van Moerb(alsem). Unsigned, no mark, first part of the 17th century. Privately owned.

De Twee Scheepjes (1750–89) and *De Porceleyne Schotel (from 1723 until after 1800)*

These two factories should be considered together since they were managed and developed with great energy by three generations of the Pennis family. From 1723 until 1763 Johannes Sr directed De Porceleyne Schotel. In that year he sold the factory to Johannes van Duyn. Simultaneously he and his son Anthony had been owners of De Twee Scheepjes since April 15, 1750. Johannes Pennis Sr died after April 26, 1774, while his son Anthony died before July 4, 1770. Anthony's widow made the business over to her son Johannes Jr in 1780. The latter must have died before May 1789 because a 'compagnie' was founded in that month. The marks used are IP and AP (Marks 124 (?) and 126, 127, 135).

Of Johannes Sr's work we know an ornamental plate depicting a smithy, one of a series of plates representing various trades which enjoyed as much popularity after 1750 as the plates representing the months of the year manufactured in De Bijl and De Lampetkan. Johannes Jr made sauce-boats with lids shaped like pikes similar to the dishes for butter and for fish manufactured in De Witte Starre; in other words, objects for daily use which were much in demand.

Anthony Pennis's talent manifested itself mainly in his technical skill. Occasionally damaged or broken Chinese porcelain—in particular lids of jars and vases—were replaced by Delft faience. Thus Anthony Pennis made two blue 'bussepotten' (cylindrical jars) to match a set of Chinese porcelain

Ill. 151. Bowl with gadrooned rim, so-called 'schilpcom' (shell-rim bowl). No mark, c. 1700. Arnhem, Gemeente Museum.

Ill. 152. Beer jug with silver lid and base rim. No mark, *c.* 1700. Amsterdam, Rijksmuseum.

(Plate XX). They are signed with his mark and are perfect in workmanship. He was also one of the most significant artists of his generation in the making of polychrome human and animal figurines (*ill. 142*).

The same can be said of Johannes van der Duyn (Marks 136, 137) who worked in De Porceleyne Schotel until his death in 1777. He was particularly adept at turning his knowledge of the faience of the best period to good account. The motifs of the small candlestick (*ill. 143*) are reminiscent of Kakiemon decoration. The careful shaping of his human and animal figurines is on a level with that of Anthony Pennis while he relies on the hues customarily used at that time, namely blue-green, rust-red and manganese on yellow background (*ill. 144*).

De Witte Starre (1723—1804)

From 1723 to 1741 this factory belonged to Cornelison Janson Brouwer (Marks 142, 143) who, together with his successor, Albertus Kiell (1761—72), contributed to making eighteenth-century faience widely known. In the period 1741—61 the factory was the property of the Van den Berg or Bergh family, which also took over its administration in 1772 as co-owner; however none of the objects they manufactured are known. In 1803 De Witte Starre became a company like other factories but it seems to have been dissolved in 1804.

Ill. 154. Two figures on horseback. No mark, *c.* 1750. Privately
owned.

A pair of sconces in impressive Louis xivth style has been preserved from the time of Cornelis Brouwer; these pieces can still be considered to belong to the classical period of Delft faience (*ill. 145*). Objects made by Albertus Kiell (Mark 144) can still frequently be found. They are characteristic of the faience of the late period; sometimes they are a combination of an object for daily use and a figurine (*ill. 146*). He certainly enjoyed popularity of a kind, but he never stood out above the average and the rather coarse quality of his time.

In the case of unsigned pieces the original design may be so accomplished in style that it works in favour of the object, as in the case of the polychrome French shoes (*ill. 147*), the two Saxon figurines (*ill. 148*) and the brightly coloured vertical fruit garland which is reminiscent of the heavy Dutch baroque art (*ill. 149*).

XII. White Delft Faience: 1600–1800

White faience constitutes a distinct group of its own. (The term 'wit goet' was used in connection with majolica, but only for the purpose of distinguishing it from reddish-brown stoneware with a tin glaze.) In the seventeenth century white faience was mainly used for housewares although some ornamental pieces were manufactured. This is apparent from inventories in which 'witte aerde kannetjes, bordetgens, commen, boterschotelen, suyckerpotten, roomkannen en tafelborden' (1624) as well as 'twee witte aerde leeuwtjes, 1 witte aerde paert' are listed (white earthenware jugs, small plates, bowls, butter dishes, sugar bowls, cream pitchers and plates—two white earthenware lions, one white earthenware horse). In spite of the blue labelling, apothecary jars are also considered to be white faience. A sirup pitcher with a handle and a cartouche bearing the inscription 'S(iroop) van Moerbal(sem)' may serve as a particularly beautiful example (*ill. 150*).

The dual purpose of these dishes and bowls is made even more plain when they are mentioned in the factory inventories: '17 aerde pronckschotelen so groot als cleyn' (1620), 'witte aerde schaalen voor de schoorsteen' (1651), 'een rack met 4 schilpcommen' (1665), 'acht witte schalen met rubbens' (1670), 'tien grote schotelen zoo voor de schoorsteenmantel, bedstee als ander ...' (1678)—(17 earthenware bowls for ceremonials, both large and small—white earthenware bowls for the mantle—a wall rack with four shell-rim bowls—eight white dishes with curved rims—ten large bowls for the mantle as well as for the bed alcove). In other words, these objects were meant both for everyday use and for ornamentation (*ill. 151*).

White jugs with large openings were meant for beer, those with narrow necks for wine. They were made either with silver or with tin lids: '1 wit kannetge met zilveren litgen' (1664), '27 witte so bier als wijnpintkannen mit tinnen leden' (1666)—(1 white jug with a silver lid—27 white beer or wine jugs with lids made of tin). Besides the smooth jugs, there are also some with a slightly wavy surface whose shape gives a particular sheen to the glaze just as in the case of the shell-rim bowls (*ill. 152*). They have been reproduced in masterly fashion by the painters of Delft; it is right that one should speak of 'Vermeer' or 'Pieter de Hoogh' jugs to this day.

While the blue, eighteenth-century snuff boxes with copper lids usually have a factory mark, the white faience boxes are almost always unsigned. A rare example of this type, which is related to the square, polychrome tea caddies (see *ill. 129*) is the tall white box for snuff with the cursive inscription 'Professers Snuyf' and a crown (*ill. 153*). The lipped rim permits us to conclude that it was closed with parchment or a pig's bladder. This in turn allows us to date the box from before 1700.

A special branch of white faience is constituted by children's dishes and by kitchenware for the dolls' rooms which were very popular at the time; six of them are still exhibited in museums. They consist of eighteenth-century cupboards which contain completely furnished houses and inhabitants when one opens the doors. Today they are invaluable cultural documents. The factory inventories give us some idea of the quantity of toys manufactured, although the meaning of the nomenclature is not always clear. Thus they mention '1 poppe aerde kanneborretgen (rek) met aerde kannetgens' (1665), '50 dosijn poppegoet' (1667 in De Vergulde Blompot), 'een back poppegoet' (1692, in the inheritance left by Rochus Hoppesteyn)—(1 earthenware wall rack with earthenware jugs—50 dozen doll playthings—one cupboard containing toys).

Human and animal figurines were also made of white faience about 1750. The factories attempted to imitate German and French porcelain by making white cows and horses and even whole groups and *genre* pictures. Because of the basic difference between faience and porcelain this attempt could not be completely successful; porcelain is considerably harder than the more brittle faience. Characteristic of this late white faience are: groups of figures on horseback based on a German design (*ill. 154*), the charming figure of a child holding a bird cage after a drawing by François Boucher (*ill. 155*) and the Dutch representation of a small child in a large canopied bed which must have been made about 1800 (*ill. 156*).

Ill. 156. Canopied bed with small child. No mark, *c.* 1800. Delft, Het Prinsenhof Museum.

DELFT POTTERIES AND CERAMIC MARKS

This list also contains data concerning the years in which the potteries began production and the years in which they closed. The illustrations of the marks are on pages 157–61.

1. *De 3 Vergulde Astonnekens*   *1655–October 15, 1803*   *Marks 1–9*

   According to a document dated October 23, 1807, a house was sold which 'voorheen geweest zijnde een plateelbakkerij "De 3 Vergulde Astonnekens"' (which was formerly the pottery factory 'De 3 Vergulde Astonnekens').

2. *De Vergulde Bloempot*   *1654–before the month*   *Marks 10–12*
   of August 1841

   The heirs of Pieter Verburgh (d. November 9, 1789) sold this factory, which from January 10, 1806 on was known as Erven Verburgh en Compagnie and became the firm Terburg Perk en Compagnie after August 20, 1813. A document dated August 12, 1841 states: 'De geinteresseerden in de Plateelbakkerij De Bloempot verkoopen percolen behoorende tot de gewezen compagnieschap van de Plateelbakkerij De Bloempot, laatstelyk geexerceerd op de Firma van der Perk en Co.' (The partners in De Bloempot factory are selling property which belongs to the former company of the factory and which was administered of late by the firm van der Perk en Co.)

3. *De Vergulde Boot*   *1634–March 13, 1770*   *Marks 13, 14*

   At present we do not know any of the objects made in this pottery. Dirck van der Kest (monogram DVK) was its manager from 1698 to 1701. In 1764, Iohan den Appel, also a manager, registered his mark (I. DA.). On March 13, 1770, the factory was bought by Dr. Willem van Blommesteijn, a councillor and lay assessor of the city of Delft.

4. *De Porceleyne Bijl*   *1657–April 29, 1803*   *Marks 15–19*

   After the sale of the factory by Hugo Brouwer in 1788, no information is to be found in the records about later owners.

5. *China*   *1654–October 5, 1743*   *No known marks*

   We do not know any of the objects made in this pottery. On October 5, 1743, Wilhelmina Toornburgh, the widow of Jacob Mesch, made a contract with the 'Directeurs en adsistenten respectieve van alle de plateelbakkerijen binnen Delft' (directors or rather the representatives of the pottery factories within the city of Delft) in order to dismantle the factory.

6. *De Porceleyne Claeuw*   *1658–September 14, 1840*   *Marks 20–26*

   On January 31, 1806 Lambertus Sanderus (d. June 18, 1813) sold '15/20 portien' (15/20 of the shares) to a company in which he himself retained 5/20 of the shares. The firm continued under the name Sanderus and Co. On November 20, 1822, his sons sold their shares to the firm which in turn, on September 14, 1840 sold 'de gewezen plateelbakkerij de Klaauw aan . . . de tegenwoordige deelhebbers van de nog bestaande compagniieschap der plateelbakkerij "de drie Klokken" (J. van Putten en Co.) (the former de Klaauw factory to the present partners in the still existing company of De drie Klokken factory).

It should be mentioned here that in 1909 H. Havard attributed the initials LVS erroneously to Liesbeth van Schoonhoven. She died in 1711, but the plates signed LVS are in the 'famille verte' style and could therefore only have been manufactured twenty years after her death.

7. *De Dissel*	*1640—November 28, 1701*	*Marks 27—32*

The administration of the 'geabandonneerde boedel' (abandoned property) belonging to this factory was the task of De Grieksche A from 1694 until all the remaining stock was taken over by it completely in 1701. On November 28, 1701, Judith van Eenhoorn sold the factory to Jacobus de Caluwe (d. 1730), a 'theepottjesbacker', who manufactured red teapots until after 1711. Later the building reverted to its original use as a brewery.

8. *De Porceleyne Fles*	*1653—1804*	*Marks 33—40*
Firm a Piccardt & Co.	*1804—1876*	*41*
Ir. Joost Thooft &	*1876—1884*	*42*
Labouchere	*1884—1903*	*42*
NV Delftsch Aardewerkfabriek		
'De Porceleyne Fles' v/h Joost Thooft &		
Labouchere	*1903—1919*	*43*
NV Koninklijke Delftsch-Aardewerk		
Fabriek 'De Porceleyne Fles'	*1919 to date*	*44*

De Porceleyne Fles is the only old Delft pottery which has been able to survive to this day. Jacobus and Dirck Harlees were among its last owners in the 18th century. The latter sold the factory in 1804 for 5,600 florins to H. A. Piccardt. After the death of the latter, his daughter Geertruida Christina managed to weather a difficult period which lasted until 1876. She was a 'Fabriekante van vuurvaste steenen en aardewark' (manufacturer of ovenproof stones and stoneware). The faience of the 1800s was influenced by Wedgwood stoneware, more durable both in material and glaze. English potters worked in Delft and thus brought 'Engelsche steen' (English stoneware) onto the market. There even was a change-over to 'gedrukte decor' (printed decoration) which was very popular in England although it had almost no success in Holland. The traditional, proven method of painting the design on the faience was unused for a long time. To maintain the firm at all, even building materials were produced. The Delft faience of that period is of very poor quality. The year 1876 can be considered as the turning point owing to the enterprise of Joost Thooft and A. Labouchere. Blue Delft faience was given new life. However, at no time was it intended to retain the old technique which could not hold its own against porcelain. The new Delft faience is essentially different from the Delft produced during the 17th and 18th centuries, in spite of the fact that, as far as shape and decoration are concerned, much was retained. After 1900, the renaissance of Delft was stimulated more and more by tourism, while at the same time De Porceleyne Fles showed great understanding of modern international ceramics and for technical, as well as artistic, experiments. In recent years building ceramics have constituted a large part of its production. In 1903, the firm became a shareholders' company and in 1919 it was permitted to add the word 'royal' to its name.

The factory mark was registered in 1883. It consists of the outline of a bottle, the monogram JT (Joost Thooft) beneath it and the name Delft written in script. This form was modified somewhat in 1903, while the products of recent years have the letter 'n' written in script on the bottle.

9. *De Drye Porceleyne Flesschen*   *1661—1777*   *Marks 16—19 and 45*

The factory was sold by the widow of Justus Brouwer and Hugo Brouwer on March 14, 1777. On December 6 of the same year a part of the 'gewezen plateelbakkerij de drie Flesschen' (former factory de drie Flesschen) was sold by the new owners.

10. *'t Fortuyn*   *1661—1791*   *Marks 46—51*

This factory was sold as early as 1791 and a 'koornwijnbranderij' (corn liquor distillery) was set up in it.

11. *Frederik van Frijtom*   *in Delft from 1658 on;*   *Marks 52, 53*
                                      died 1702

An artist who worked independently and made mainly blue plaques and plates decorated with landscapes.

12. *De Grieksche A*   *1658—after 1818*   *Marks 54—73*

On December 10, 1811 the widow of Pieter van Marxveld sold the factory to Joost Vrijdag who founded a company 'De Eendragt' together with the firm Ley, Bellard en Comp. 'tot het fabriceeren van Plateelbakkers- of Delftsch aardewerk en. z. g. Engelsch aardewerk . . .' (In order to manufacture earthenware of faience or so-called English stoneware). The new company began its activity on January 1, 1812. The merged companies De Grieksche A and De Endraagt were still mentioned in 1818.

13. *De Ham*   *1639—before 1726*   *No known marks*

None of the products of this factory are known. A document dated April 10, 1726 refers to the 'mortificatie en tenietdoening van de gewezen plateelbakkerij Den Ham' (striking of the former De Ham factory from the register).

14. *'t Hart*   *1661 — after 1762*   *Marks 74—78*

How long this factory continued to function after 1762 is not known.

15. *De 4 Romeinsche Helden*   *before 1616–after 1738*   *No known marks*

On July 20, 1742 Joris Verlengh sold 'het overgebleven gedeelte van de gewezen plateelbak-kerij, van ouds gen. de vier Romeinsche Helden . . . de gen. plateelbakkerij zal ten allen tijde moeten zijn en blijven gemortificeerd' (the part of the factory which has been preserved; the factory, which has always been called 'De 4 Romeinsche Helden', must for all time be strik-en and remain striken from the register).

16. *Het Hooge Huys*   *1648–1741*   *No known marks*

The factory was sold by Franciscus Ferrier on June 19, 1741 and there was a condition that it 'moet voor 1 Augustus 1741 afgebroken zijn' (must be dismantled before August 1, 1741).

17. *Het Lage Huys* (see also *Rouaen*)   *1714–March 19, 1742*   *No known marks*

On December 1, 1714 the Rouaen factory was bought by two 'mr. goutschilders' of De Griek-sche A, Jan Franson Schoonjan and Lodewijk van der Horst. From then on they called the factory Het Lage Huys. In 1722, Van der Horst made over his share to Schoonjan, who man-aged the business as sole owner until 1735. On April 20, 1735 he sold it to Paulus van Essen who, on March 19, 1742 disposed of 'het overblijfsel van de gewezen plateelbakkerij van ouds genaamd Rouaen' (the remains of the former Rouaen factory, as it was called of old). Further data about the fate of the factory are lacking.

18. *De Drye Clocken*   *1670–1841*   *Marks 79–84*

A company was founded in 1809 in the name of Jacobus van der Putten. On September 14, 1840 De Claeuw was also taken into the firm. On September 17, 1841 the factory buildings were sold by 'als tegenwoordig eenig overgeblevene deelhabbers in de Compagnie de drie Klokken (Firma J. v. d. Putten) aan het Koninkrijk der Nederlanden . . .' (by the only remain-ing partners in the firm J. v. d. Putten to the Kingdom of the Netherlands).

19. *De Porceleyne Lampetkan*   *1637–1811*   *Marks 85–90*

In January 1810, the widow of Abraham van der Ceel-Vierkant left the utensils and stock of this establishment to her nephew Hendrik van der Ceel Courou, who lived in the house which belonged to the factory. The business was sold on October 21, 1811; the new owners were not potters.

20. *Het Jonge Moriaenshooft*   *1654–1792*   *Marks 91–96*

21. *Het Oude Moriaenshooft*   *before 1690–1792*   *Mark 97*

On May 31, 1772 both factories became the property of Cornelis and Thomas Fonteyn. The former left them both to his brother in a will dated July 10, 1782. Thomas sold them on July 30, 1792 as 'Fabricquen van Engelsch Steen en Delftsche Aardewerk'. As early as Sep-tember 11, 1793 Het Oude and Het Jonge Moriaenshooft were being 'vertimmerd tot een dobbelde koornwijnbranderij' (transformed into a double corn liquor distillery).

22. *De Paeuw*   *1651—1779*   *Marks 98—105*

The 'gewezen plateelbakkerij de Paeuw' (the former De Paeuw factory) is mentioned in a document dated October 26, 1779.

23. *Het Gecroond Porceleyn*   *1648—1753*   *No known marks*

According to a document dated December 20, 1753 'De Directeuren van de Plateelbakkerijen binnen Delft verkoopen het gecroond Porceleyn' (the directors of the pottery factories in Delft are selling het gecroond Porceleyn). The buyers of the factory were obliged 'te doen afbreken zonder dat zij of opvolgende eigenaars het gekochte mogen aanlegen of employeeren tot een plateelbakkerij' (to demolish it, without permission for themselves or future owners to en-large or operate the acquired property as a pottery factory).

24. *De Metalen Pot*   *1638—after January 1, 1757 Marks 106—114*

This pottery was sold on September 15, 1756 to Pieter Paree. He probably was still its owner when the mark MP was registered for De Metalen Pot in 1756; however nothing further is known about this factory at present.

25. *De Romeyn*   *1613—after June 6, 1769*   *Marks 115, 116*

The last owners were Petrus van Marum (1754—64) and Jan van der Kloot Jr (1764—67). Immediately after that, the factory was taken over by a company, but that was dissolved as early as June 6, 1769. Later Jan der Windt was its sole owner. Nothing further is known about him.

26. *De Roos*   *1666—before*   *Marks 117—123*
                                January 30, 1858

After April 13, 1755, Dirck van der Does was the owner of this factory which manufactured faience and tiles. His 'geabandonnerd boedel' (abandoned property) was sold in 1770. Diffi-cult years followed, until the city government gave assistance to the factory: 'Geassocieerden en Directeurs exerceerende in de tegelbakkerij ... Mr. Hendrik van der Goes, Secretaris der Stad. 29 Juli 1812 Mr. Cornelis van der Goes van Naters. Op 24 Februari 1816 woordt de te-gelbakkerij voortgezet als Firma van der Goes en Comp.' (Partners and directors who admin-ister the factory ... Mr Hendrik van der Goes, City secretary. On July 29, 1812 Mr Cor-nelis van der Goes van Naters. After the 24th of February 1816, the factory continues as the firm Van der Goes and Co). The heirs of Willem van der Goes (d. before July 27, 1841) sold the tile factory on October 8 and 15, 1841 to Mr J. M. van der Mandele. On January 30, 1858 he sold 'een huis ... met de daarachter gelegen gebouwen en getimmerten, worin vroeger de tegelbakkerij genaamd de Roos is uitgeoefend' (a house with buildings and sheds in which the tile factory by the name of De Roos used to be located in the past).

27. *Rouaen* (see also Het Lage Huys)   *before 1603—1714*   *No known marks*

| 28. | *De Twee Scheepjes* | *before 1653—before* | *Marks 124—127* |
| | | *May 18, 1796* | |

This factory was managed by three generations of the Pennis family (1750—89). A company was founded on May 16, 1789 which passed into other hands in 1794. A document dated May 18, 1796 refers to the 'gewezen plateelbakkerij Het Scheepje'.

| 29. | *De Dobbelde Schenckan* | *1661—1777* | *Marks 128—134* |

A document dated August 25, 1777 mentions 'de gewezen plateelbakkerij De Schenckan'.

| 30. | *De Porceleyne Schotel* | *after 1612—1800* | *Marks 135—137* |

Ysbrand van Duijn, who died on September 15, 1800, is thought to have been the last owner of De Porceleyne Schotel. To date nothing is known about the liquidation of the factory.

| 31. | *De Witte Starre* | *1660—1804* | *Marks 138—144* |

This factory was owned by the De Bergh or Van den Bergh family from April 4, 1741. It was taken over by a company on March 10, 1803; however, in a document dated October 15, 1804, reference was already made to 'de gewezen plateelbakkerij De Witte Starre'.

32.	*De Wildemanspoort*	*1661—1681*	*No known marks*
	later given the name		
	De Twee Wildemannen	*1681—1794*	*Mark 145*

In spite of the many names under which this factory was known since it was founded, none of the works of the artists associated with it are known. Willem van Beek, 'plateelschilder' bought the business on January 14, 1760 and registered his mark in 1764. None of his works are known either. According to a document dated January 14, 1794, Agatha Harlees sold 'en huis en erve, zijnde voorheen geweest de plateelbakkerij "De Wildemans"' (a house, a garden and a piece of land which used to belong to De Wildemans factory).
(The Harlees family is also mentioned above in connection with *De Porceleyne Fles*.)

| 33. | *Monogram LVS* | | *Marks 146, 147* |
| | (see *De Porceleyne Claeuw*) | | |

| 34. | *De Gecroonde Theepot* | | *Mark 148* |

1 1679-1705	2 1700-1705	3 1700-1705	4 1705-1712	5 1718-1757	6 1718-1735
7 1764	8 1757-1803	9 1757-1803	10 1734-1764	11 1734-1764	12 1764
13 	14 1764	15 1739-1775	16 1760-1788	17 1739-1788	18 1739-1788
19 	20 1661-1695	21 1712-1763	22 1712-1763	23 1712-1763	
24 1739-1763	25 1764-1806	26 1840-1850	27 1650-1694	28 1650-1694	29 1650- nach 1700
30 1694-1697	31 1694-1697	32 1694-1697	33 1697-1701	34 1697-1701	35 1697-1701

36 1697-1701	37 1764	38 1771-1786	39 1771-1786	40 1786-1804	41 DICCARDT DELFT 1804-1876
42 nach 1883	43 DELFT nach 1903	44 Delft nach 1903	45 HB H8 2 1760-1788	46 jhES 1661-1691	47 Fortuin 1706-1764
48 Fortuin 1706-1791	49 t Fortuin 1706-1791		50 J:H:F 1185 in t fortuiyn 1762-1791		51 WVDB 1764
52 F.v. FRYTOM 1684	53 f.v.frijtom 1692	54 F I r SE 10 1674-1686		55 SE 1674-1686	56 AK AK 1686-1701
57 AK AK ca 1700	58 AK ca 1700	59 AK 1701-1722	60 APK 1711 1701-1722	61 APK 1701-1722	62 JvDH JvDH 1703-1722
63 JvDH 1703-1722	64 j.w:H 1) 1703-1722	65 A ITD 1758-1764	66 A D 12 1758-1764	67 DEX 1758-1764	68 A :H 1764

158

69	70	71	72	73	74
1764	1764-1768	1764-1768	1768-1785	1785-1811	1661-1686
75	76	77	78	79	80
1686-1745	ca 1700	1675-1693	1762-?	1675-1693	1686-1745
81	82	83	84	85	86
1706-1725	1725-1764	1764	1809-1840	1723-1743	1743-1756
87	88	89	90	91	92
1756-1778	1778-1811	1778-1811	1778-1811	1654-1671	1671-1692
93	94	95	96	97	98
1671-1692	1689	1692-1730	1692-1730	1761-1769	1662-1679
99	100	101	102	103
1667-1691	1701-1705	1705-1725	1705-1725	1725-1740

104 jVH 1730	105 paam 1740 IDM. 1740-1769	106 4K 1662-1679	107 ⱻ Ꜫ 1667-1691	108 VE 6 0 1691-1721
109 VE 8 0 HK 1691-1721				
110 VE 7 3 ⱽP 1691-1722	111 VE 10 3 1691-1722 ⚹P	112 VE 6 0 1691-1721?	113 VE 5 2 MP 1721-1764?	114 MP. 1764
115 PM. 1754-1764	116 W 1764-1767	117 ᛏ R. 1673-1680 -1694 ?	118 S. R. 1694-1712	119 H·S·s R. 1694-1712
120 R 1694-1712				
121 Roos Roos 1727-1755	122 Roos G. 1727-1755	123 DVD ❀ 1755-1770	124 R 1691?	125 J:G 48 1707-1725
126 P P 1750-1774				
127 AP 3 AR 1759-1782	128 VE 8 5 iP n°6 9 1688-1713	129 VE 4 0 P° VE 2 0 DS 1688-1713	130 DS 1704	131 VE IK 4 1688-1713
132 VE 10 1688-1713				
133 GDK HDK 1721	134 DSK 1764	135 P. P 1750-1763	136 Duyn 1763-1777	137 1782-1800
138 4K 1660-1671				

139	140	141	142	143	144
Ɛ	✳	✦ 112	CB ✳	✳ CB	✳ AK AK ✳
1687-1689	1705-1723	1705-1723	1723-1741	1723-1741	1764

145	146	147	148	
W:V:B	LVS	LVS		
1764	ca 1730	ca 1730	1671-1708	

General Index

(The references in italic numerals are to illustrations, those in roman numerals are to colour plates.)

Index of Personal Names

(The references in italic numbers are to illustrations, those in roman to colour plates.)

Index of Marks

(The references in italic numerals are to illustrations, those in roman numerals are to colour plates.)

PK	Pieter Kam XIII
R, r, Roos	De Roos 62, *54*, *80*
RIHS	Rochus Hoppesteyn 72, *65*, *66*
SVE	Samuel van Eenhoorn 43, *36*, *42*, *43*
V Duyn	Johannes van Duyn *143*, *144*
VR	Ary van Rijsselberg 120, *122*
	(See AR above)
WVD	Willem van der Does 140
WVDB	Widow van den Briel 134
Z. Dex/Z. Dextra	Zacharius Dextra 118, *117*
Z. E.	37

Select Bibliography

Berendsen, A., *et al.*	*Tiles*, London 1967
Fourest, H. P.	*Les Faïences de Delft*, in the series 'L'œil du Connaisseur', 1957
Gelder, H. E. van	*Glas en Ceramiek, De Kunsten van het vuur*, 1915
Havard, H.	*Catalogue des Faïences de Delft composant la Collection de Mr. John F. Loudon*, 1877
Havard, H.	*La Céramique hollandaise*, 1909
Havard, H.	*La Fayence de Delft*, 1878
Helbig, J.	*Faïences hollandaises*
Hoynck van Papendrecht, A.	*De Rotterdamsche Plateel- en Tegelbakkers en hun Product, 1590—1851*, 1920
Hudig, F. W.	*Delfter Fayence*, 1929
Jonge, C. H. de	*Oud-Nederlandsche Majolica en Delftsch Aardewerk*, Amsterdam 1947
Korf, D.	*Dutch Tiles*, London 1963
Korf, D.	*Nederlandse Majolica*, 1963
Knowles, W. Pitcairn	*Dutch Pottery and Porcelain*, 1913
Lunsingh Scheurleer, T. H.	*Sprekend Verleden, Wegwijzer voor de verzamelaar van oude kunst en antiek*, 1959
Neurdenburg, M. E. and Rackham, B.	*Old Dutch Pottery and Tiles*, London 1923
Ottema, N.	*Friesche Majolica*, 1920
Ottema, N.	*De beginperiode van de Friesche Majolica*, 1926
Paape, G.	*De Plateelbakker of Delftsch Aardewerk Maaker*, 1794
Picolpasso, Cipriano	*Li tre Libri dell'Arte del Vasaio*, 1548
Rackham, Bernard	*Early Netherlands Maiolica*, London 1926
Ray, Anthony	*Early Delftware Pottery in the Robert Hall Warren Collection*, London 1968
Santos Simões, J. M. dos	*Carreaux Céramiques Hollandais au Portugal et en Espagne*, 1959
Vecht, A.	*Frederich van Frijtom*, Amsterdam 1968
Vis, E. M., de Geus, C., and Hudig, F. W.	*Althollandische Fliesen*, 2nd edn 1933
Visser, M. A. de	'Rood steenen trekpotjes met het merk "Ary de Milde"', in *Oudheidkundig Jaarboek*, 1927
Visser, M. A. de	*Zie verder Tijdschriften: Oud-Holland*, 1957
Westers, A.	*Gedateerde voorwerpen van oud-Nederlandse Majolica*, 1963
Wittop Koning, D. A.	*Delftse Apotherspotten*, 1954